GREATNESS IN
MUSIC

Da Capo Press Music Reprint Series

GENERAL EDITOR

FREDERICK FREEDMAN

VASSAR COLLEGE

GREATNESS IN
MUSIC

By Alfred Einstein

Translated by César Saerchinger

DA CAPO PRESS · NEW YORK · 1972

Library of Congress Cataloging in Publication Data
Einstein, Alfred, 1880-1952.
   Greatness in music.
   (Da Capo Press music reprint series)
   Translation of Grösse in der Musik.
   1. Music—Philosophy and aesthetics. 2. Genius.
I. Title.
ML3847.E4813   1972   780.1   70-87527
ISBN 0-306-71441-8

This Da Capo Press edition of *Greatness in Music is an*
unabridged republication of the first edition published
in New York in 1941. It is reprinted by special arrangement
with Miss Eva H. Einstein.

Published by Da Capo Press, Inc.
A Subsidiary of Plenum Publishing Corporation
227 West 17th Street, New York, New York 10011

Manufactured in the United States of America

GREATNESS IN MUSIC

GREATNESS IN
MUSIC

o o o o o o o o o o o o o o o o o o o

ALFRED EINSTEIN
TRANSLATED BY CÉSAR SAERCHINGER

OXFORD UNIVERSITY PRESS
NEW YORK   LONDON   TORONTO
1941

Preface

○ ○

THE AUTHOR of these reflections on the conditions for greatness in music is, by avocation, what has in recent years come to be called—in America and even in England—a musicologist. But the exigencies of life have also led him, over a long stretch of years, to exercise the function of a music critic. This dual activity has had the consequence that his musicological colleagues regard him, for the most part, as a passable critic, and his critical colleagues have, for the most part, pronounced him a passable scholar.

Whatever the truth may be, he himself is not dissatisfied with his lot. As a critic he has been able to regard contemporary phenomena a little *sub specie æternitatis;* while as a musicologist he was always prevented from lapsing entirely into 'musical philology,' into dry scientific research. And in dealing with the past and its great representatives, he has

PREFACE

applied not merely an 'objective' curiosity, but always a vital and vitally changing interest. 'Objectivity' has appeared to him always as an ideal difficult to realize—and sometimes as just a beautiful word. Perhaps only Minos, the judge of the dead, can be really objective.

In this book the reader will note the traces of this dual activity, which may be a single one after all. It was written after the completion of an extensive and purely scientific work—a history of the Italian madrigal and its subsidiary forms which, thanks to its extraordinary proportions, has not yet achieved publication. The writing of the present volume, requiring no long preliminary research, no copious scientific equipment, and no learned annotations was, so to speak, a recreation. It is not long; but it may be pertinent to remember that a French writer once apologized for the great length of one of his books by saying that 'he hadn't the time to be brief.' True, this one was written in a short time, but it is nevertheless the result of considerable experience and long preoccupation with the great masters. In a few of its sections it takes the form of variations on thoughts already recorded by the author in his critical effusions. Its general stimulus came from the

PREFACE

chapter on historical greatness in Jacob Burckhardt's *Weltgeschichtliche Betrachtungen* (*Observations on World History*), a book to be recommended to all who are humanistically inclined as especially elevating in these times of moral and intellectual upheaval or atrophy.

The author has spoken as freely and critically of the great masters of music as though they were still living and subjects of dispute. Some people may resent this. For example, it will be easy to accuse him, by citing passages torn from their context, of lack of reverence for Wagner, or even of animosity towards him. It will also be easy to find contradictions between the opinions and judgments given in these pages and those contained in the little *History of Music* which he once wrote for teaching purposes, and which also has been translated into English. No one is to be deprived of these pastimes. But it is hoped that, nevertheless, some readers may feel that the compelling motives in writing this book were reverence, gratitude, and love.

Northampton, Massachusetts,
    1 *June* 1941.

Contents

I

Questionable Greatness

Why, I'm posterity—and so are you;
  And whom do we remember? Not a hundred.
Were every memory written down all true,
  The tenth or twentieth name would be but blundered;
Even Plutarch's Lives have but pick'd out a few,
  And 'gainst those few your annalists have thunder'd;
And Mitford in the nineteenth century
Gives, with Greek truth, the good old Greek the lie.
                    BYRON, *Don Juan*, xii, 19.

$\mathcal{I}$N Munich, where I was born, there is still in use today a concert hall of classical style—the Great Odeon Hall—with a wide apse for the orchestra, in the semi-circle of which are a number of round niches, filled with busts of musicians. They are of plaster; materially and artistically their value is nil. But the interesting thing about them is that they have constantly changed. In 1811, when the Odeon was new, Michael Haydn still stood beside Joseph Haydn. Cimarosa was in Beethoven's place, and I am not sure whether Bach already figured by the side of Handel or—more likely—Jommelli or Hasse. While I was still young, about 1890, there were ten plaster heads: Bach and Handel, Gluck and Haydn, Mozart and Beethoven, Weber and Schubert, Schumann and Mendelssohn —a choice with which in those days one might to some extent agree. But when Felix Mottl—a con-

(3)

ductor who once awakened an Indian Summer in the heart of Cosima Wagner—came to Munich, he increased the illustrious crescent by two further busts: Wagner and Liszt. Brahms did not come into consideration, presumably because his bearded face would have appeared strange among all those more or less classic Roman masks. What the collection is like today, I don't know: I only suspect that Mendelssohn has vanished and that Anton Bruckner has moved into his place.

Thus shifts the valuation of greatness within little more than a hundred years; and whoever needs further proof of its mutability need only read what Giuseppe Carpani has to say in his book on Haydn (shockingly plundered by Stendhal, alias 'Monsieur Bombet') about his idol as a composer of operas. He says, quite rightly, that in this field Haydn has been far surpassed by predecessors and contemporaries. And then he cites as *'giganti della musica teatrale,'* as 'giants of opera,' a long list of names in which we find those of Predieri, Borroni, Bonomi, Borghi, Nasolini, and Tarchi—names about which the present author (and probably the esteemed reader) can inform himself only by means of an encyclopedia— while that of Gluck is missing. Well, Carpani was a little man and survives only in the wake of Haydn and Stendhal. Already we have seen that our judgment of greatness is obscured not only by nationalistic blinkers, but also by proximity in time. And, as a matter of fact, there are types of greatness in all arts, but especially in poetry and music, that are unable to reach beyond certain geographical borders or periods of time. We shall have to remember this later on.

But in some cases posterity has a way of disregarding even the opinions of its own idols. In a letter to Hans von Bülow, of 29 November 1856, Richard Wagner declared that he considered Liszt's *Orpheus* to be 'an altogether unique work of the highest perfection.' This opinion would be open to suspicion if it had been addressed to Liszt. But to his disciple, Hans von Bülow, Wagner did not use to be hypocritical, at least not at this time. It would be difficult for the public of today to prove the correctness of Wagner's evaluation of *Orpheus,* for there is hardly a conductor who now puts it on his programs. And yet it seems that Wagner's recommendation ought to carry some weight!

o 2 o

NEVERTHELESS, artistic greatness is both more permanent and universal than historical greatness. Only
rarely is historical greatness unchallenged, and all
the more rarely the closer to us the figure of the
'great man' stands. And even the most remote figures may lose their nimbus; they may be dethroned
by history, by a change in opinion. Was Alexander
the Great really great, or was he just a conqueror?
Julius Caesar ranks as a really great man, although
we do not speak of him as 'Caesar the Great'; for
'the great' is an epithet which, curiously enough, is
reserved chiefly for monarchs and popes. But his contemporaries and the next generation saw him, in the
dim light of party passion, as the grave-digger of
Roman freedom; for practical reasons they preferred
to idolize the living. Was Frederick the Great great?
Austrian historians always had difficulty in admitting it; just as some Berlin and London contemporaries—for instance, Sir Walter Scott—had difficulty
in admitting the greatness of Napoleon, both before
and after the battles of Leipzig and Waterloo. Historical greatness is always confined within national

(6)

boundaries; it took the objective vision of a Goethe immediately to recognize the greatness of Napoleon, and to preserve the memory of a conversation with him as one of the great moments of his life.

Is greatness, or rather the acknowledgment of greatness, in art really more lasting and less subject to change? One hesitates to say yes. One remembers —to cite an example from the graphic arts—the dispute which has gone on since the middle of the sixteenth century among the artists in Rome, about who was greater, Raphael or Michelangelo. We today are inclined to consider that it has been decided in favor of Michelangelo; but perhaps it will never be really decided, because it is not subject to decision. Here enters what one might call 'elective affinity,' or the affinity of periods—that curious fluctuation of taste between that which excites and that which calms, between the Apollonic and the Dionysian. The attitude of the period to the great masters changes with every generation, and whenever there occurs a pause, a balance of opinions, then the 'great man' affected by this condition is removed into the sphere of the monumental, which is equivalent to petrification, or death. It is possible that a portion of the art of Johann Sebastian Bach might become the victim of such petrification. We concede that such art is great; but it no longer concerns us. If there were no great men who permit us to see constantly changing facets of their greatness, we should not need to be interested in the past except from a philological or scientific point of view.

We ourselves, within our short existence, experience a similar change—a change which may develop into that state of petrification. Our personal relation to the great masters, too, is fluid, restless, comparable to one who loves—or hates. Lucky, if it does not end in apathy! To me and the generation to which I belong, Wagner is the best example of this changing taste. About 1890, ten years after his death, the effectiveness of Wagner's work had reached its highest peak in Germany. He had completely conquered us and the world; he had become effective in the way he wanted: he had given us something in place of life—that is, he had provided us (as someone has so happily put it) with a substitute for our emotions; he created the intoxication which lifted us out of ourselves. He falsified and shifted the entire function of art in life. After the great intoxication came the great sobering-up. The period between 1910 and 1930 could be described

negatively as the period of revulsion against Wagner
—nationally and internationally. But when the effect of this reaction, too, had evaporated; when
Wagner's music emerged, so to say, from the process
of purification; behold! the admiration for Wagner,
the *artist,* grew again to immeasurable heights. It
will be a long time yet before he is abandoned to indifference, or petrification. Even today every musician, and not only musicians, professes an opinion
regarding him.

° 3 °

PETRIFICATION is the state of all art which no longer
affects us, even though it has proved its historical
importance. We know that Dufay, Josquin, Gombert, Clemens non Papa, Palestrina, Lasso, Monteverdi were great masters—some of them not only in
a historical sense but also by absolute standards. But
—there is no mistaking it—they can no longer be
made to 'live,' to make a direct appeal to the popular mind. There are too many preliminary requirements before one can 'get the feel' of a Dufay chan-
son, a Josquin motet, a Gombert mass, a Lasso
madrigal, of Monteverdi's *Orfeo* or *Incoronazione di
Poppea.* Only the few who fill the requirements can

perceive the 'eternal' that is present in these works: their compelling and unfading humanity and artistry. Those few are the artists, and thus indirectly it is possible to bring to life even the work of the masters who are, so to say, great 'on credit.' Or, to risk another comparison: the artists who bring back to our memory the work of a forgotten master (ill-treated by time) are very much like Voltaire, who, although he could not restore the tortured Jean Calas to life, was able to vindicate his memory —and at any rate add a new laurel to *his* own crown of fame. Bach's work had survived in the work of every master, in Mozart, Beethoven, Wagner, Brahms (in each according to his own style), before the general public became aware of Bach's own greatness once more. Brahms has brought to life— and made us understand—segments of the seventeenth, the sixteenth, and even a bit of the fifteenth century—for instance, in the finale of the E-minor symphony, in the motets, and even in some of the songs—without conductors, choruses, singers or listeners being aware of it. They accept all this as samples of Brahms's oddity. There is an enormous mass of dead music, and its volume increases daily;

(10)

but there is also a good portion that is only seemingly dead; and this—in order to live—needs only a master's magic words: 'Arise and walk!'

On the other hand, there is a great mass of apparently live music that is in reality dead. It is claimed that the great musician has been recognized by his contemporaries, or at least by a good proportion of them; that none, at any rate, has gone without acclaim. That is not true, either in music or in any other of the arts. It availed Schubert little to have Beethoven exclaim on his sick bed, after looking through several songs: 'Truly, in him glows the divine spark.' Without Schumann's *Neue Zeitschrift für Musik*, without Liszt's transcriptions, Schubert would have remained a Viennese local light for several decades more. One must grow very old—seventy-five, like Sibelius—to have his contemporaries place him on a level with Beethoven. Which is in any case too soon. On the other hand, one may grow just as old, seventy-five and more, like Richard Strauss, and outlive his own fame—to become a figure in history.

◦ 4 ◦

AND even if the statement that every great man is recognized during his lifetime were true, one would have to ask: *how* recognized; with what degree of recognition? How was it with Bach? I shall not labor the point of how much he was or was not recognized. One knows that when Johann Kuhnau, the cantor of St. Thomas's School, died in Leipzig in 1722, the Council of the worthy city turned first to Telemann and Graupner, two very good but certainly not great musicians. And it was only when Telemann declined and Graupner could not obtain a release from his sovereign prince in Hesse that they approached Bach, whereupon one councilman, whose name deserves eternal fame, delivered himself of this utterance: 'Since one cannot have the best, one must be satisfied with the middling.' The man of whom this was said was nearly forty years old and he had written the Inventions and the Symphonies, the first part of the *Well-tempered Clavichord*, the *Chromatic Fantasy*, the Brandenburg Concertos, the *Little Organ Book* and a few of his greatest Preludes and Fugues for organ. One cannot argue that Bach was, alas! unknown and that his works were not printed. The works were distributed in manuscript copies. Bach had already made a number of tours, during which he had played his own works; and since he had entered upon the duties of his post in Leipzig—a city famous for its annual Trade Fair, and sometimes known as 'Little Paris'—hundreds of people every Sunday had the opportunity of hearing his cantatas and Passions. But they heard nothing—in the true sense. Johann Adolf Scheibe, the prototype of the intellectual critic who like so many of his modern successors would have made a better lawyer than musician, called him (in his *Critische Musicus*) the 'Lohenstein of music,' thus comparing him with the most insipid representative of the pompous baroque poets of the time. This was after Bach had written his Passions, the B-minor Mass, the *Magnificat,* and several hundred of his cantatas.

Bach the creator was never understood, let alone recognized, during his lifetime. He achieved his peak of public appreciation only as an organist and organizing conductor. J. M. Gessner, the rector of St. Thomas's School, praises him in an explanatory note to an edition of *Quinctilianus* as a pianist, organist, and choir-master: 'I am otherwise a great

admirer of antiquity, but I believe that my friend
Bach, and whoever may resemble him, comprises
within himself many men like Orpheus and twenty
singers like Arion.' *Et si quis illi similis sit forte!*
This man, who stood so close to Bach never once
felt the unique qualities of Bach's creations. And
one must not think that Frederick the Great, when
he invited Bach to Potsdam in 1741, possessed a
better standard for valuing his true greatness, his
powers of creation, or anything beyond his mastery
of the contrapuntal handicraft. To him, who played
and wrote such 'gallant' flute concertos, 'Old Bach'
was a polyphonic fossil, a fabled dinosaur of the distant musical past. And even in 1826, Hans Georg
Naegeli, a Swiss publisher and musician, permitted
to be printed in his *Lectures on Music, with Particular Regard to the Amateur* (page 126): 'In
Bach's time people recognized no greatness in art
except just that greatness of contrapuntal art.' When
the same Naegeli published Beethoven's three sonatas, opus 31, as an 'Original Edition,' he allowed
himself to slip in three bars at the end of the first
movement of the one in G major, a proceeding
which was not exactly edifying to Beethoven: 'His
astonishment and anger, when he saw it printed like

that, are hard to imagine.' This is the respect that a colleague had for the greatest genius of his time.

What was the state of Beethoven's recognition by his contemporaries? Yes, Beethoven was a recognized and successful composer. No musician has engaged the world's attention during his lifetime more than he; no other composer's works have created a greater sensation. He himself saw deeper, as witness this anecdote, contained in the memoirs of J. von Seyfried, the truth of which was vouched for by a contemporary. 'Once, when Beethoven had already had the most flattering proofs of his recognition in England, he sat in the "Golden Lamb" in Vienna and noticed that a number of musicians and literary men were engaged in a lively conversation. He asked one of them what was up. "These gentlemen claim that the English know neither how to perform good music nor how to appreciate it," answered Mayseder, "but I have a different opinion." Beethoven said sarcastically: "The English have ordered several compositions from me for their concerts and have offered me a handsome fee; the Germans, with the exception of the Viennese, have only just begun to perform my works; and the French find my music unplayable. Therefore it is as clear as day that the

English understand nothing about music. Isn't that so?" ' The tragi-comic note of this story lies in the fact that—Beethoven to the contrary notwithstanding—the English knew as little about the real Beethoven as did the Germans (including the Viennese), the French, and the rest of the world.

° 5 °

THE admiring press notices that Beethoven received during his lifetime were characteristic of his time rather than appropriate to his works. Even the most intelligent among them—that of the poet-musician E. T. A. Hoffmann—is no exception, with its mixture of high-flown romanticism and dry Berlinese technicality. Only one real poet, Grillparzer, had an inkling of Beethoven's greatness, and found the right words for it—in his funeral oration: 'He was an artist; and what he was, he was only through his art. He was an artist, but also a human being, a human being in every sense and the highest. Because he shut himself off from the world, men called him hostile, and because he avoided sentimentality, they called him unfeeling. Oh, he who knows himself to be hard does not flee. The finest points are the most easily blunted, or bent, or broken. Excess of sensibility must beware of sentiment. He fled the world because, in the wide range of his loving heart he found no weapon with which to resist it. He withdrew from mankind after he had given it everything and had received nothing in return . . .' The first of the different periods of Beethoven's posthumous fame begins with this grave-side speech.

They are just so many periods of partial understanding, or distorted understanding. There is the Beethoven of Schumann, of Berlioz, of Liszt, and of Wagner: each has a different aspect; each portrait contradicts the others, just like the actual portraits of Beethoven that have been preserved—*et adhuc sub judice lis est.* That Beethoven could—and can—endure all these variations is a negative proof of his greatness. He is greater than his time and all the succeeding times. And as it is with him, so it is with all other great musicians. In an article on the characteristics of the various keys, written by Robert Schumann—yes, Schumann!—the author sees nothing in Mozart's G-minor symphony but 'ethereal Grecian grace' (*schwebende griechische Grazie*)! The fact that Mozart has been able to survive, unscathed, the adulation of the Empire, Biedermeier, and Romantic periods, is but one token of his immortality.

o 6 o

'IMMORTALITY.' We know now that this is a questionable concept, in art as in history. But this concept varies according to the different arts. It is curious that here, too, music is like architecture, with which it is so often compared: architecture as 'frozen music'; and music as architecture projected into the flow of time. The most durable masterpieces are the works of architecture; and this by no means refers to the material, but to the works as creations—the Pyramid of Cheops, the Temple to Poseidon at Pæstum, the dome of the Pantheon. Sculpture and painting are of more limited duration, and their evaluation more subject to change. In the debate over 'absolute value,' the older, more monumental sculpture of Egypt seems just now to have triumphed over the Hermes of Praxiteles; just as El Greco has triumphed over Velasquez, and Tintoretto over Titian—which in the course of a generation may have changed once again, in response to a new 'affinity.' Poetry appears to be the shortest-lived among the arts—and not only the shortest-lived but also the most restricted in its 'international' influence, owing to its dependence on the national tongue. The higher a piece of poetry ranks as a masterpiece of speech, the less translatable it is. Shelley and Keats mean nothing to the Germans; Hölderlin and Mörike nothing to the French. What is left of the greatest lyric poems—even of a dramatic work like Goethe's *Faust*—when it is bereft of the magic of its verse?

But quite apart from this dependence on the national speech (a geographical limitation) poetry is badly off. Its most precious flowers resemble certain climatically restricted plants that do not survive after transplantation from north to south, or from south to north. The lesser products, which *do* permit transplantation—the, let us say commoner, less noble species—are the shortest-lived. A theatrical manager estimates the average life-span of a play at sixty days; a publisher reckons ninety days for a new novel. If the play or the book does not become profitable within this period, it is a 'dud'—a fiasco. It is dead and will never be resurrected—never, unless by means of other successful, more 'permanent' works the author manages to arouse some interest in such stepchildren of his success.

° 7 °

MUSIC is better off, because music is absolutely inconceivable without form. Form in art is the means of conservation, of keeping alive. Therefore poetry is more permanent than prose, an epic more 'eternal' than a novel (unless the prose of the novel has been *formed*—shaped down to the last word, as in Flaubert's *Madame Bovary*). This accounts for the yearning after artistic form, even on the part of scholars and scientists, such as Lucretius Carus when he wrote his didactic poem *On the Nature of Things,* or Fracastoro, when he penned his *De morbo Gallico.*

Firmness and stability are of the very essence of music, as is shown by the most elementary facts. If we play three chords, one after the other—the dominant, tonic, sub-dominant—it is certainly a possible sequence, but from the point of view of content a rather unstable one. However, if we take the sequence: tonic, sub-dominant, dominant, tonic, it suddenly becomes complete, rounded, riveted. It becomes a little building—like the tower of Sant'Apollinare in Classe, near Ravenna—so perfect and stable that even an earthquake·could not shake it. And what is true of the elementary forms is even truer of the higher types. To me Bach's Inventions and Symphonies have always seemed to be the most 'eternal' pieces in the whole literature of music—so perfect that not a single note could be altered without damage to the whole work; as perfect and precious as a string of sapphires cut by a master. By comparison with these 'little things' ('Little Things Can Also Charm Us,' according to Number 1 of Hugo Wolf's *Italian Song-Book*), the best-formed larger works of music seem merely like chased gold. To what attributes do Beethoven's sonata movements owe their 'immortality'? Not so much to their content; not always to the mighty personality behind them. This personality is behind *every* work of Beethoven's. For example, behind his *Choral Fantasy*, opus 80, for piano, orchestra, and chorus, whose impulses are as powerful as those of the Finale of the *Ninth Symphony*. But there the form is too loose, the blocks are too unchiselled. And so the *Choral Fantasy* has remained only a stepping stone to that Finale, which has itself been regarded as a failure by a great many good musicians—such as Verdi, for example—and often still is. No, Beethoven's greatness does not lie in the fact that he excelled Haydn and Mozart, that he filled prepared forms with more powerful matter, but in the fact that *for* this more powerful material, this stronger impulse, he sought a more powerful *form*. Why did he write three Leonore overtures? Because the *form* of the first two did not satisfy him. It will hardly even be possible to settle the dispute about whether he preferred the second or the third. The second is the bolder and, programmatically, the more logical. The third, in its *reprise,* adds a conventional and formalistic touch, but has, at the same time, the firmer mold. It is clearer. To Beethoven the overture, though by its nature 'program music,' was not *only* program music, as it was to Weber. Why are there a dozen or more programmatic interpretations for the *Eroica*— none of which is right or even convincing? Because Beethoven wanted to offer the highest achievement in form-creation, and did present the highest that was attainable. This program music is beyond all programs. It could be much clearer, in the sense of poetic interpretation, but it would be just that much weaker and less clear as music.

o 8 o

IN art there is no 'eternity.' Even Horace predicted only a *comparative* permanence for his hammered and chiselled poetry, written in the most enduring of all languages—the language of a great Empire which in his day gave promise of an incalculable duration. '*Ære perennius,*' he said: 'more lasting than ore'— and thus suggested a *degree* of permanence. As a matter of fact, words are more lasting than ore and stone. Formed tone is more lasting than words, and not only more lasting but more directly effective—across all national barriers.

Across all? That is far too rhetorical. Music is at a disadvantage, as against poetry, to this extent: it need not be translated, but—neither is it susceptible of translation. A good translation makes it possible for us to penetrate to the furthest and remotest religions and literatures: to the Book of Job, one of the most magnificent pieces of oriental poetry; to the thought-complex of Chinese wisdom, not to mention Chinese painting and sculpture. In music the barrier between European and oriental music is impassable—from both sides. There may be a few exceptions, but they prove the rule. European music represents, moreover, only a very restricted phase in a prodigious development. The concept 'European music' is equivalent to the following: polyphonic music; harmonically interpretable music; harmony with a melodic contour; melody on a harmonic base. The nineteenth century has attempted to harmonize oriental music—Chinese, Arabian, Polynesian, and Gregorian singing, and each attempt has resulted in a violation. Genuine monodic music and genuine harmonic music are as incompatible as fire and water.

<h2 style="text-align:center">∘ 9 ∘</h2>

THE common saying that music is a universal language, generally intelligible—the application of which we tacitly limit to *European* music—is, after all, only a saying. We cannot, of course, subscribe to the theory and practice of the race fanatics—people who, while they do not altogether deny to the French or British some knowledge of, and general approach to, Beethoven, nevertheless deny to them the profounder understanding of the 'German' master. These people have driven Mendelssohn from the German concert hall as a 'Near-Easterner,' and would eliminate Heinrich Heine from the history of German literature—while they do not shy at appropriating Shakespeare to themselves. How singular! Beethoven entrusted the first performance of his *Kreutzer Sonata* to a mulatto; and Carl Maria von Weber, next to Wagner the most 'German' of all masters, made not the slightest objection to having a Mr. Braham, alias Abraham, sing the part of Hüon in the world première of *Oberon*. The interpretation of Beethoven's last quartets which made the deepest and strongest impression upon me was that of the Frenchman Capet and his colleagues, and the greatest performer of Bach's Partitas and Beethoven's sonatas is the Catalan cellist, Pablo Casals. But in music, too, there are insurmountable barriers between nations. The greatness of a master, the regional ties and national 'dialect' of a musician have no part in this, whatever.

To speak first of the 'regional' qualities of the musicians belonging to the younger nations: national color is to the music of certain masters no obstacle to universal appeal. On the contrary, it is a kind of vehicle. It is the Czech element in the music of Smetana and Dvořák that enhances its attractiveness, though it is certainly not Czech color alone

(25)

that constitutes its value and charm. It is the Russian flavor of Borodin, Moussorgsky, and Rimsky-Korsakov that gave their works the wings with which they spanned the earth, though it was not the Russian flavor alone. Edward Grieg is an internationally recognized—and justifiably recognized—minor poet, because his music is strongly Norwegian in character, not in spite of it. When Schubert begins to adopt a Hungarian dialect, it only adds to his charm, but it must be Schubert who speaks the dialect. Even second-hand music—such as Hungarian Rhapsodies by Liszt or Hungarian Dances by Brahms—gains international popularity when it dons a national costume, as it were. And the most detestable music is immediately identified and recognized when it bears a Spanish or Neapolitan or Nordic stamp.

o   IO   o

THE noblest example of the blending of national and international greatness is, of course, Frédéric François Chopin. This blending is so intimate, so esoteric, that the Polish, the French, and the German ingredients are indistinguishable, because they are transmuted into Chopinesque. Yes, even the German.

QUESTIONABLE GREATNESS

There is Bach and Mozart in Chopin's music, but it is wholly dissolved and absorbed: it may be sensed, as austerity and charm, by our delight in it, though it may defy our analysis. Even in the Mazurkas and Polonaises there is Bach and Mozart; and that lifts it beyond all national limitations: Chopin's 'national' music is always universal music as well. Who is ever reminded of Poland by listening to the B-minor sonata? Who, when hearing Chopin's Nocturnes, ever thinks of Paris or Vallombrosa—or wherever else there are nights and stars? Once (1 October 1848) Chopin wrote jokingly to his friend, Count Grzymala: 'Soon I shall forget the Polish language, shall speak French and English; and I shall learn English with a Scottish accent and be transformed into Old Jaworek, who spoke in five languages at the same time!' In reality—as a musician—he neither forgot his Polish, nor learned French or English, nor did he speak in five languages at once, but always only in one, namely his own. Since his works exist, our idea of Polish music is determined by him, and not vice versa.

○ II ○

ON the other hand—or, rather, contrariwise—a
'universal' master does not benefit from his universality in the least: nations that are closely related in
race and language may have very different attitudes
to such a master. Mozart is a good example of this.
Mozart's music is super-national; it has no 'coloring.' Indeed it is sometimes Salzburgian, sometimes
Strassburgian, sometimes Viennese—as a joke, for
special effect. But wherever Mozart is serious—and
music is to him the only serious affair in life—he
speaks no dialect, only the purest language in the
world. It is no Esperanto, no international speech-
currency. It is Mozartian language—the clearest,
brightest, most transparent speech in the music of
the second half of the eighteenth century, distilled
from a myriad of sounds, conceived by the finest ear
and the most critical taste that is recorded in the
entire history of music. It is, to use a favorite expression of Goethe's from the realm of alchemy, 'co-
hobated' music. Well, this Mozart has found the
most loving comprehension in the country which he
personally liked least, among the nation with the

(28)

best taste, the nation with the greatest attachment to tradition—the French. In view of this fact one is reminded of a conversational remark by Goethe (8 July 1825) about the French, which speaks 'of their great attainments in the cultivation of language and thought, of their *naïveté,* their child-likeness which survives even their most extreme sophistications.' The same exactly might be said of Mozart. It is no accident that Mozart's piano sonatas and concertos are played best by Frenchmen, and that the best Mozart biography has been written in French. Bach is to some extent accepted in Italy, even Beethoven, even . . . Brahms, and certainly Wagner; Mozart, however, is impossible. Not despite the fact of his having written three of his master works to Italian libretti, but because of it. They had no success in the Italy of their period; they have no success today. Not a reasonable word about Mozart is to be found in Italian literature on music, because he leaves the Italians 'cold,' in the most literal sense of the word. In Verdi's letters the name of Mozart does not even appear. Yes, once! In 1871, when Verdi was offered the chairmanship of a commission for the reform of music-teaching, he casually mentions Gluck and Mozart among those who offered their respects to Padre Martini in Bologna! And in 1878 he mentions without disapproval the fact that Haydn and Mozart had come near to 'the Italian attributes' (*le nostre qualità*) and yet remained *quartettisti*. That's it: *quartettisti*—instrumental composers. We, however, see in Mozart a model and ideal of the *cantabile* style, while the Italian fails to recognize this vocal quality—which is the vocal quality of a Cimarosa, a Rossini, a Bellini, and a Verdi. But it does not follow that the cantabile style of Mozart is inferior to the racy cantabile of a Neapolitan folk-singer. So we see that neither the national costume, nor so-called internationalism, nor super-nationalism have anything to do with world-wide validity in music. Both can be either an obstacle or an advantage. Nor does 'greatness' play a decisive part; for Mozart certainly is indisputably a great composer, and Grieg just as indisputably not a great but—to express it uncharitably and unjustly —a *little* 'mannerist,' a lesser *genre* painter in tones.

II

Unquestionable Greatness

> . . . *Most frequently the measuring*
> *of genius is still regarded as a crime.*
> NIETZSCHE, *Dawn*,
> Aphorism 548.

*I*N order to determine greatness in music one places a group—larger or smaller, according to the standard to be applied—in the foreground, behind which the lesser figures more or less disappear in the shadow. But one must immediately eliminate 'historical' greatness, and greatness which is circumscribed by national boundaries. In a certain modern Dictionary a number of special articles are devoted to musicians who certainly must have been thought worthy of the honor for reasons connected with their significance. I set down their names in the fortuitous helter-skelter sequence determined by the alphabetical order of the authors of the articles, and I want to emphasize that no criticism, in the customary sense, is intended. On the contrary, this selection is a valuable historical document for the determination of what was considered important in and about the year 1940. Well, the

sequence is as follows: Rimsky-Korsakov, Richard
Strauss, Sullivan, Vaughan Williams, Bach, Boro-
din, Moussorgsky, Delius, Berlioz, Falla, d'Indy,
Ravel, Saint-Saëns, Gluck, Busoni, Palestrina, Sibe-
lius, Weber, Loeffler, Bruckner, Mahler, Bartók,
Hindemith, Kodály, Respighi, Pizzetti, Haydn,
Purcell, Grieg, Mendelssohn, Křének, Brahms,
MacDowell, Rachmaninoff, Malipiero, Szyman-
owski, Franck, Handel, Byrd, Elgar, Schumann,
Tchaikovsky, Chopin, Wolf, Schubert, Monteverdi,
Alban Berg, Mozart, Rossini, Beethoven, Liszt,
Stravinsky, Dvořák, Janaček, Schönberg, Smetana,
Wagner, Debussy, Puccini, Verdi.

It is hardly possible to contemplate this list without pleasure and profit, and think about it for hours:
every name is a problem. Let us disregard the mod-
erns and ultra-moderns, in the selection of whose
names the indispensable considerations of international courtesy has played a part. For instance, where
Respighi, the composer of the brutal *Feste di Roma*
and the still more brutal *Lucrezia,* is represented, a
dozen finer musicians from each of twenty nations
would surely have the right to be considered. But
—let us be tolerant. We know little about the degree
of 'mortality' and 'immortality' of the musicians of

our time, and not our time alone but the time of our fathers and grandfathers as well. Hatred of the fathers and their ideals is inborn and natural to youth; youth must be unjust, must underestimate its elders. And along with these ideals—say, the ideals of romanticism—goes all music of the past that is, or seems to be, related to romanticism: thus with Wagner goes not only Weber but also Beethoven, who can so easily be seen and interpreted in a Wagnerian light. The youth of 1920 leapt across Beethoven to Bach, whom it presumably sees in a false light, too.

o 2 o

SIMILARLY, let us exclude the musicians of the centuries before the appearance of Bach and Handel. Guillaume Dufay and Josquin were great masters and tomorrow may be such again; but the popular Dictionary would have difficulty in explaining their greatness to its readers. But, if one includes Byrd and Palestrina, why not Lasso, Clemens non Papa, Cipriano Rore—not to mention many another name? Palestrina's greatness is largely a legend, which may be proved true only by a real history of sixteenth-century music. And if Monteverdi, why not Schütz,

Lully, Buxtehude? If Purcell, why not Couperin 'le Grand,' Domenico Scarlatti, and Pergolesi?

Some of the other names, too, are denied the attribute of international greatness, indisputably acknowledged. Let me repeat: the degree, the intensity of national coloring plays only a very unimportant role in this. Moussorgsky, the 'most Russian of all Russian composers,' has traversed the frontiers of his home-land without resistance; his *Boris Godounov,* his song cycles, may be understood differently in London, in Berlin, in Rome, and in New York, but they are none the less understood. Moreover, this understanding, or this love, does not depend upon the Russian 'color,' upon the folksong flavor, as it often does in other cases—Hungarian, Czech, Spanish. Rather do we glimpse through their Russianism the deep humanness of the *Nursery,* of the *Songs and Dances of Death.* These are Russian children and people, but above all they are children and people. And when we have recognized this, we have come a little closer to the secret of their greatness.

Not even the possibility of an imitation detracts from this international, super-national effectiveness. Moussorgsky is inimitable: not even in Germany, the most colorless of all musical countries, can anyone compose *à la* Moussorgsky. Chopin, on the other hand, is the most easily imitated composer; he can be imitated, and has been imitated, by composers regardless of their place of birth— Leipzig or the Government of Novgorov, Paris or Barcelona, Copenhagen or Montevideo.

o 3 o

BUT in other cases the national barrier is insurmountable. Only in England itself can one learn and estimate what Elgar means to England—not to mention Vaughan Williams; while in Germany he is just one musician among many, a British mixture of the lesser progeny of Wagner, Liszt, and Brahms. To English ears he is the peer of Brahms, and it is difficult to make this credible to a German. Brahms himself, a world figure everywhere in the northern lands, is nothing more than a respectable musician in the south, notably in Italy—despite Martucci and other stray admirers. It is characteristic that throughout Verdi's correspondence the name Brahms does not occur, at least not in connection with music, although Brahms was a zealous theater-goer, and a passionate admirer of Bizet's *Carmen,* among other things. Another, and very curious case, is that of Anton Bruckner, whom many people in Germany and Austria secretly or openly place far above Beethoven—as Beethoven's 'consummator,' after having been placed, during his lifetime, 'only' above Brahms—the members of the Viennese Wagner Society, for instance; the critic, Hugo Wolf. In Anglo-Saxon countries—and in Latin countries, including Wagnerized France—Bruckner does not even come into consideration, and meets with absolute lack of understanding, with the coolest and most callous indifference. Here Bruckner is considered as formally weak; but one of his greatest alleged weaknesses, his manner of breaking off one section of a movement and with seeming irrelevance beginning another, is considered by an intelligent Swabian admirer (August Halm: *Von zwei Kulturen der Musik,* p. 138) as a virtue—as 'the grandiose honesty of his Grand Pauses.' Halm argues like this: the sonata (more accurately sonata form) requires 'times' (more accurately passages, transitions)—times which are devoted to the 'recovery from one event and the gathering of forces for the next.' These passages, he says, are 'apparently formless, but actually loaded with form . . .' Well, while with the classics very little happens in such places, with Bruckner nothing happens at all. The decisive question is, simply, whether such a 'grandiosely honest Grand Pause' in Bruckner is really loaded with form, or whether it isn't just empty— in other words, a hole. In Germany people accept the first alternative, in England the second.

o 4 o

SINCE the seventeenth century when rivalry in music began, at least between Italian and French music, we are worse off than the people of earlier times. Dufay and Josquin were international, super-national musicians; Victoria was a Spanish but at the same time a Roman composer. Since the nineteenth century, since every nation has contributed to the construction of the musical tower, the Babylonian confusion has reached immeasurable heights. Music has begun to speak dialects, which even within a common national or geographical frame are no longer understood by all. In South America there is, perhaps, Chilean, Peruvian, Bolivian, Ecuadorian, and Colombian—and certainly Argentinian and Brazilian music; presumably there are Mexican, Costa Rican, and Nicaraguan musicians in Central America. And within the former political entity known as Yugoslavia there is Croatian, Serbian, and Slovenian music—each about as 'distinct' from the others as Bavarian music would be from Swabian.

° 5 °

WE shall come still nearer to the concept of greatness in music, the concept of unquestionable greatness, if we test the sound of some of the names that are 'recognized' in musical history—Bach and Handel, Gluck and Haydn, Mozart and Beethoven, Weber and Schubert, Schumann and Mendelssohn, Wagner and Liszt, Berlioz and Verdi—not to mention others. Weber? Does he belong in this sequence—the sequence Bach-Mozart-Beethoven? It seems strange to us that the boundaries of his life are contained within those of Beethoven, that he was born sixteen years—only sixteen years—after him, and that he died a year before him. One need but compare Beethoven's only opera, *Fidelio,* with the only really successful one of Weber, *Freischütz,* in order to appreciate the difference. *Fidelio,* according to its style, is not a German (or 'Teuton') opera at all, but an *opéra comique;* and the libretto may easily be translated back into French, without loss of quality. More than that, the music will lose nothing by any sort of 'translation' in the world; it is, in the true sense of the word, the music of humanity. *Der Freischütz* is subject to ridicule on every stage except the German. The national significance of *Freischütz* and its composer is hardly to be overestimated; but the reverse is true of its international importance. Weber suffers from the fact that Richard Wagner, in his oration at Weber's final resting place, asserted that 'a more German musician had never lived.' (Is there a comparative form, or a superlative one, of 'German'? Wagner did not realize that he thus negated the race principle, for he did not know that Weber's grandmother, née Chelard, was French.) 'Behold! today the Briton does you justice, the Frenchman admires you, but only the German can love you; you are his, a beautiful day in his life, a warm drop of his blood, a segment of his heart . . .' If that is true, it proves the German theater-going public's tolerance of borrowed forms; for the famous *Wolfsschlucht* music is a French *mélodrame,* Ännchen's romanza is a

French *romance,* and the great Scene and Aria of Agathe is an Italian *scena.*

But this does not dispose of the case of Weber. He must possess qualities which justify, or at least explain, his inclusion among the great Ten or Twelve. The explanation may, perhaps, be found in the fact that he incarnates a different kind of musicianship than that which existed before. In him musicianship is blended with new powers of personality. As a musician, he is far more universal than the musicians of the century near the end of which he was born: he was a piano virtuoso, a conductor (conductor in an entirely new sense!), an opera director, a critic, a writer, and a poet. He had a dangerous versatility of talent, similar to that of his literary contemporary, E. T. A. Hoffmann—a versatility that does not culminate in poetic gifts, as with Hoffmann, but in music, and that culminates much more decidedly with him than with Hoffmann, who was so cleft, so torn, so inhibited by his gifts. Weber succeeded: although forced by a mountebank father to be a prodigy; although passed from teacher to teacher without learning anything worth while; although he abandoned his musical avocation for the sake of a courtly post, until a domestic catastrophe matured him as an artist and a man, he finally managed to land his ship in a safe harbor, without fear of becoming a Philistine. He had to deal with life quite differently from his colleagues; as with Mozart and Beethoven, it was more difficult for him just because he no longer ran true to type—was not a legitimate member of the guild. Mozart was ruined by this leap into freedom; Weber triumphed in spite of it.

Weber is the first musician of the nineteenth century, the prototype of the species. The appearance of Anton Bruckner—who was born two years before Weber's death, in the first quarter of the nineteenth century—is so miraculous because once again there suddenly seemed to arise a guild-musician of the eighteenth century—quite 'un-literary,' naive, unsuited to his environment and age. Not that this new mixture of personality, however uniformly directed, did not weaken his musical activity—or, more correctly, limit it to a definite direction. Weber's contemporaries' ears were sensitive to the novel, the strange, the unprofessional in him. It is a matter of record how that musical quietist, Franz Grillparzer, the Austrian poet, raised in the spirit and circle of Mozart, reacted to the *Freischütz* with dis-

pleasure—a displeasure that increased to abhorrence with the hearing of *Euryanthe.* 'This opera,' he said, 'can please only fools or idiots or pundits or street robbers or assassins.' Weber, according to him, was 'a poetic mind but no musician.' Familiar, too, is Franz Schubert's scorn of the dilettante Weber: 'This is no music, this is no Finale, no ensemble according to form and order . . . there is no idea of legitimate development, and wherever Weber wants to appear learned, one immediately discovers that he comes from the school of a charlatan *
. . . he has talent, but no solid foundation on which he could build . . . everything is aimed at mere effect . . .' One may judge the degree to which Beethoven mistrusted Weber as a musician, namely from his exclamation after hearing the *Freischütz:* 'I should never have thought him capable of it! Now let Weber write operas, one after the other, and without taking any too much trouble over it (. . . *ohne viel daran zu knaupeln*)!' In other words, just so he won't write any more symphonies, concertos, or sonatas!

Indeed, Weber's whole creative effort was henceforth devoted to opera. Of course, he wrote piano

* Abbé Vogler.

works, chamber music, masses, concertos and songs as well. Outwardly the thematic catalogue of his works, which Friedrich Wilhelm Jaehns published in 1871, looks like the Koechel Catalogue of the works of Mozart. Yet no one cites the *Freischütz* as Jaehns No. 277, or the *Invitation to the Dance* as Jaehns No. 260. Nor will this ever be different. About twenty years ago a Complete Edition of the works of Weber was projected; but it never matured beyond two or three scanty volumes. And even if it should ever be completed, and should acquaint us with a series of hitherto wholly or partly unavailable works, it would not shift the basis of our judgment of Weber. It would be about the same as if, after one hundred years, one were to arrange for a Complete Edition of Leoncavallo and Mascagni for the sake of *Pagliacci* and *Cavalleria Rusticana;* or—to choose a comparison more worthy of Weber—to publish a Complete Bizet Edition for the sake of *Carmen.*

Why is it that a Weber song cannot hold a candle to one of Schubert's? Why is it that his Variations for Piano cannot be compared with Mozart's, from which they derive, and still less with Beethoven's? Why is it that his piano sonatas seem to belong to a different—more shallow—period than those of Beethoven? It is partly because these songs bear the *cachet* of the folksong, and also because they are imitations; partly they are 'dramatic' songs, sung by the 'protagonist'—in any case not genuinely lyrical. And his instrumental works suffer from a fatal approach—from the side of virtuosity and the 'brilliant.' Beethoven is often very difficult to play, but never 'brilliant.' Even Weber's 'brilliance' still belongs to the virtuoso's age of innocence: it is still naive, gay, direct. But it is already the brilliance of the nineteenth century, which Schumann or Chopin were to overcome or, rather, sublimate—and not without effort. It is the brilliance that was to be further developed by Liszt; it is not without significance that Weber's Concert-Stück in F minor was one of the show-pieces of Liszt's youth.

This brilliance spoiled Weber as a composer of chamber music and as a symphonist. His works are never symphonically conceived. Indeed, the *concertante* style is in his blood. And that is why his major instrumental works are in this field: a quintet, a duo with obbligato clarinet, and a few concertos for the clarinet, which he has, as it were, re-discovered after Mozart. No one else has so thoroughly devoted himself to the singing quality of this instrument. Compared with Weber's, the instrumentation of Beethoven has an air of being old-fashioned and stereotyped. And, one may say, he would not have been Weber if he had 'learned' more—in the academic sense. He would certainly not have become Weber the dramatist had he not been gifted with that peculiar, emphatic—even penetrating—melodiousness which is the source of the brilliance mentioned above. His melody is of an indisputable and unmistakable originality; it is already present in full strength in the *Six petites Pièces faciles* of 1801, and persists in undiminished vitality through to *Oberon*. This 'penetrating' melody has its root in a deliberate system of 'exaggeration,' to which Weber once confessed quite openly in speaking to a younger colleague, Lobe by name.

This system is not particularly attractive in his instrumental music; but in his operas it is not merely legitimate—it is the secret of their effectiveness. What Schubert disliked—as being calculated for effect—is of the very essence of opera. Without his 'search for effect' Weber could never have been that which in Germany is the Phoenix of all Phoenixes —a genuine opera composer. Opera, especially

German romantic opera, which was set on its feet
when Mozart wrote the *Magic Flute,* may be a bad
thing; but once it had become a fact there was nothing more to be gained for it by 'restraint,' by 'art.'
It is by no means an accident that Beethoven wrote
no further operas after *Fidelio,* despite his zest for
it and despite good subjects—for instance *Macbeth.*
Nor was anything to be gained by just instinct;
only by conscious effort. The *Freischütz,* which
nevertheless took Weber four years to compose,
stands at the point where Weber's inspiration and
his conscious effort are about equally balanced. Once
again, as at various times in the course of operatic
history, the issue of the day was *unity* in opera; and
Weber achieved this unity, and conquered it, without worrying much about the disparity of the
sources from which it flowed. So great was the characterization of his melody, so new and powerful the
musical impression which he drew from the color and
the mood of his subject. The same, or similar, processes are repeated in *Euryanthe* and *Oberon,* but in
Euryanthe the balance has already ominously shifted
to the side of conscious effort; and in any case
Oberon, bewitching in its color, is only the sketch
for a maturer version, which Weber was prevented

from writing by his untimely death. *Euryanthe*, the
first German *opera seria*, Wagnerian before the time
of Wagner, is a style-creation in the realm of program music, an experiment that shows traces of ex-
cessive effort and strain—an effort that failed because Weber applied no symphonic principle to the
finali, yet a clairvoyant leap of genius, a sure-footed
premonitary attempt at a new balance between music and drama. Wagner was right in extravagantly
admiring Weber; he knew what he was doing when
he began his Dresden incumbency with a performance of—precisely—*Euryanthe*. Moreover, to him,
Weber was still more of a 'romantic composer' than
he is—or can be—to us; and, for that matter, more
romantic than Wagner himself.

Weber's romanticism presents a peculiar case.
Weber is not a romanticist like Eichendorff and
Novalis (to name two German poets) or Schubert
and Schumann (to name two musicians). His
music does not issue from the mystical depths of
human inwardness and spiritual absorption; he cultivates romanticism only in so far as it is compatible
with theatricalism. The worlds that Weber conquered—the macabre, the medieval-chivalrous, the
oriental, the Spanish-gypsified—are no longer ro-

mantic to us: to us they lack the nocturnal mystery, the enchantment; they have become more picturesque than they were to Weber's contemporaries. But we are compensated by a finer ear for all that is chivalrous, aristocratic, and nobly passionate in his music.

Was Weber a great musician? He has worked in all species of music, without being a universal master. He is a composer of operas. Here, again we have a single work that has proved its permanence —a work so national in feeling that it cannot be transplanted. Then we have a few sonatas, variations, polonaises, which *can* be transplanted; and the *Invitation to the Dance*. I don't know. To me it seems that in the semi-circle that holds the niches of Bach and Handel, Haydn and Mozart, Beethoven and Schubert, there should at least be distinctions in the size of the heads. The little band of the elect must not be clad in uniform.

If Weber is to be authenticated as a great master, a Czech will claim that Smetana, too, is a great master. What the *Freischütz* was—or is—to Germany, the *Bartered Bride* became to Smetana's people forty-five years later. Besides, the *Bartered Bride* has the added advantage that its libretto is not only 'romantic' and time-bound, but universally intelligible and valid; and that its music is not only Czech in color, but also Schubertian. Smetana is a proof that every nation will place its particular domestic deity among the select group of undisputed, international, super-national gods—France may be Rameau, Russia not only Moussorgsky but also Glinka, Borodin, and Rimsky-Korsakov (and all with justification), Italy perhaps Bellini; not to mention the smaller and more recent musical lands.

∘ 6 ∘

WHAT about the head of Mendelssohn? It is, of course, obvious that we must try to assign to him the correct place, to avoid the overvaluation bestowed on him during his lifetime and by the generation that came after him in Germany and England; also the undervaluation that was originated, or represented, by Wagner, and which in certain parts of Europe—*non ragionam di lor*—has increased to contempt. It might lead to a fresh overvaluation; but it would be kinder if it were to lead to a new estimate of Mendelssohn, a re-valuation based on new knowledge. For he is today one of the least-

(51)

known musicians of the past. What one knows best of his work is the least significant—the pieces that have been most often imitated by mediocre musicians because they corresponded to the bourgeois romantic taste of the time.

Wagner sought to disparage Mendelssohn even personally—for his human qualities—as far as possible, and we can hardly decide whether he was justified, or how far. What do we know about the human characteristics, about the true visage of the great men of the past? Each of these visages acquires, in the course of time, an idealized mask; and the farther removed a personality, in point of time, the more it becomes a myth. There is no portrait of Homer; but there are ancient busts of Homer, and though they are not 'natural' they are *true*, because—to use a Kantian distinction, they represent not the 'empirical' Homer, but the 'intelligible' one. So it is with all great men. The Bayreuth Wagner literature, fostered by Cosima, has for some time successfully worked to create a Wagner myth —by suppression and false interpretation of facts, by secreting and destroying documents. Wagner himself furnished the basis for this in the alleged 'plain truthfulness' of his autobiography, which it was not permitted to question even by means of proven contrary facts.

There is already a mythical Beethoven. We become aware of this when we read the account of a contemporary, who was a poet, but an incorruptible observer, namely Franz Grillparzer. 'During one of the following summers' (it must have been 1805) 'I occasionally visited my grandmother, who occupied a country dwelling in near-by Doebling. Beethoven also lived in Doebling at that time. Opposite my grandmother's windows lay the decrepit house of a peasant notorious for his slovenliness, Flehberger by name. This Flehberger also possessed, aside from his ugly house, a pretty but not very well-reputed daughter, Lise. Beethoven seemed to take much interest in the girl. I can still see him, as he ascended the Hirschengasse, the usual white handkerchief in his right hand and dragging along the ground, and stopping at Flehberger's farmyard gate, inside which the light-minded beauty stood atop a hay or dung waggon and, constantly laughing, busied herself lustily with the pitchfork. I have never noticed that Beethoven addressed her; but he stood silently and peered through the gate until finally the girl, whose taste preferred peasant lads, made him angry, either with a word of mockery or by ignoring him stubbornly. Thereupon, with a quick turn, he buzzed off suddenly, but nevertheless did not fail to stop again at the gate next time. Nay, his interest went so far that when the girl's father went to the village jail (known as the *Kotter*) on account of a drunken brawl, Beethoven intervened before the assembled village council to get him released. But in doing so, in his customary manner, he treated the worthy councillors so roughly that it needed but little to have thrown him into involuntary company with his imprisoned protégé.'

This story is much more realistic than the story of Shakespeare's poaching. We are shocked. The composer of the *Eroica*, the *Ninth Symphony* and the *Solemn Hymn of Thanksgiving offered by a Convalescent to the Deity*, in the role of silent troubadour to Lise Flehberger of Upper Doebling! But in reality only flappers and gushing adolescents can take umbrage at such an incompatibility between myth and reality. The intelligible man is important; not the empirical one.

Grillparzer was still thoroughly a man of the eighteenth century, and, as such, did not balk at describing so human a trait of Beethoven. Not till the nineteenth century did that eunuchistic school of biography begin to flourish which describes a great man as virtually without sex—a school that did not, however, hinder a most shameless type of scandalous literature from reaching its full flower. Mozart was an especially idealized, and already dandified, victim of such biographical writing, round about 1850; while the still-living Liszt, on the other hand, was the victim of that scandalmongering literature, because he left behind him a few too violently broken hearts after absolving, as Nietzsche put it, the 'school of velocity with women.' Today we suffer from a contrary evil, thanks to psychoanalysis and the vogue for a type of biography that one might call 'conjectural.' But it is certain that posterity is entitled to know everything about the life of its great ones—even the most intimate details. If they are really great, they must be able to survive it.

And what about Mendelssohn? We must look for a less suspect witness than Wagner; and for a more independent one than Goethe, who reported as follows to Zelter, after the visit of the twenty-two-year-old at Weimar: 'Just now . . . the excellent Felix . . . after spending a pleasurable fort-

night with us, and having edified everyone with his
amiable art, is off to Jena in order to delight the
kindly-disposed strangers and leave our country a
memory which must always be cherished . . . Do
say the very best to the parents of the extraordinary
young artist, and in impressive words . . .'

Our opposite witness is Ludwig Meinardus, a
German musician who entered the Leipzig Conservatory in the year of Mendelssohn's death, 1847. His
autobiography, entitled *Ein Jugendleben* (*A Life of
Youth*), is a pretty unpalatable book, but thanks to
its fidelity and love of truth a historical source-book
of the first rank. Well, his experiences with Mendelssohn were just so many collisions. The master
treats the twenty-year-old with intentional objectivity and coldness; he breaks his promise to save his
new pupil the entrance examination; after this examination he makes fun of the 'delinquent' behind
his back. During the perusal of his immature compositions, a sequence of consecutive fifths and octaves causes a storm with the sensitive master; during a subsequent examination of all the pupils,
Mendelssohn entertains the convivial faculty with
cruel caricatures of the youthful victims, including
a cripple. Meinardus openly revolted against the

director. However, it must be recounted in Mendelssohn's favor that 'this scene had no direct con-
sequences for the revolter.' But it is no excuse for
Mendelssohn to say that his innate mastery, coupled
with ineptitude, made him doubly sensitive, and
that he believed himself, thanks to his obstinacy,
immune from disagreeable duties of a conservatory
director. (Imagine Beethoven or Wagner as conservatory directors!) Let me repeat, it was the year
of Mendelssohn's death. All this is much more
characteristic than the specifically Berlinese smart
talk and lack of respect, which occasionally peep
out of the letters of Mendelssohn to his sister. On
the one side Goethe, on the other Meinardus; it is
clear that we do not yet know over-much about
Mendelssohn as an 'empirical' character. But we
know all the more about his 'intelligible' character.
The writer of the not always agreeable family letters
mentioned above is a first-class and objective deline-
ator of people and scenes. As an aestheticist he is
superior to Wagner, although he has not so great a
command of words. In a classic piece of writing,
dated 15 October 1842, he proved once for all the
absurdity of the romantic craze for the 'interpretation' of absolute music: 'To me the thoughts which

(57)

music express are not too indefinite, but too definite, to be described in words.' This is the musician who wrote the *Hebrides* overture, the octet, the scherzo in the music to *A Midsummer Night's Dream,* the violin concerto, the *Italian Symphony* and—to name only one of his vocal works—the *First Walpurgis Night* to Goethe's text (a ballad which is too 'heathenish' to find wide acceptance). One likes to speak, in connection with Mendelssohn, of 'smoothness of form'; but this, in his highest achievements, is true mastery. One likes to speak of his 'shallowness of emotion'; but this, in the most beautiful moments, amounts to captivating charm. Some blockhead or other has said that even when Mendelssohn had nothing to say, he nevertheless said it in an agreeable way. What Mendelssohn lacked, for the attainment of true greatness, is the courage to say the ultimate—in love, or in tragedy. Bear Mozart in mind, and all this is clear. Mendelssohn could write no letters like Mozart's 'Baesle' letters, which certainly is not to be regretted—he simply lived in an all-too-civilizing century. But neither could he write an aria of the frankness of Leporello's 'Register' aria in *Don Giovanni.* While Wagner was thinking about 'Siegfried's Death' and Verdi of

Macbeth, Mendelssohn was thinking about the
Loreley of the tender-souled and patriotic phrase-
maker Emanuel Geibel. But another type of musician, namely Brahms, was justified in his admiration
of Mendelssohn, when he wrote (September 1874):
'I would sacrifice all my works to have been able to
compose an overture like the *Hebrides* of Mendelssohn.'

° 7 °

THEN there is another head, concerning whose
claim to the largest dimensions stirs some doubts in
our minds, and that is Gluck. Biographically speaking, it represents a giant; it is the head of a powerful glutton and drinker, given to all the worldly
enjoyments; the head of a man of violence—a head
which Greuze has preserved for us in all its vitality.
But the product of this head has not proved its
vitality, as have those of Bach or Mozart, of Haydn
and Beethoven. For the past hundred years and
more it has always been an experiment to produce
one of the works—or, more precisely, one of the
operas—of Gluck; and none of these experiments
has led to a protracted revival of Gluck. If one asks
what it is that occasionally brings *Alceste* back to

(59)

the stage, one may find that it is the ambition of some prima donna, as for instance in Berlioz's time, when *Orfeo ed Euridice* was 're-discovered' by Pauline Viardot-Garcia. In our time its revival is, more often, due to the desperation of opera managers—managers who see in Gluck a chance to 'enrich the repertoire,' or an escape from the necessity of producing contemporary works. Or it may be the day-dream of some operatic stage-manager who sees in *Orfeo* and the two *Iphigenias* a possibility to elbow himself from the wings into the limelight. Indicative of this train of thought is the fact that two of Gluck's most characteristic operas, *Paride ed Elena* and *Echo et Narcisse* (the latter being his last opera) are invariably left out of consideration—and off the repertoire. In such 'Gluck salvages' Gluck's music plays a very minor role. And it is true that in the sense of Bach and his contemporaries, Gluck was not a great musician. There is no doubt, for instance, that Nikolaus Forkel, musical director at the University of Göttingen, who was a passionate admirer of Bach, and was his first biographer, was an equally passionate despiser of Gluck. And when the severe sister of Frederick the Great, the Princess Amalie of Prussia, had the score of

Iphigénie en Aulide submitted to her by Kirnberger, she formulated her judgment in such a classic manner that we cannot forego a quotation: 'Herr Gluck, in my opinion, will never be able to pass as a clever man in composition. He has (1) no invention at all, (2) a poor, wretched gift of melody, and (3) no accent, the whole opera is thoroughly miserable; but this is the new taste, and it has very many adherents.'

A witty contemporary of Frederick the Great, of Joseph II of Austria, and of Catherine the Great of Russia, once said: '*Un re è più o meno sempre bello.*' Thus one might say, too, that the judgment of the royal blue-stocking is more or less true, if it were not foolish and narrow-minded. Mozart, who personally was not a friend of Gluck and who (1) was a creator of the first rank, (2) possessed a magnificent melodic gift, and (3) was capable of the most profound expressiveness, would certainly not have subscribed to the royal judgment. Mozart was a secret admirer of Gluck; and he never missed a rehearsal when Gluck revived his operas in German at the Vienna Burg-Theater in the early 1780's. As a dramatic composer he learned enormously from Gluck; and even as a melodist he was most deeply stimu-

lated by him. Gluck no melodist! Gluck has written
passages of extreme melodic delicacy and perfection;
for instance, the solemn dance in the 'Tombeau' at
the opening of *Orfeo*. True, he was less gifted than
many a contemporary. He 'learned' less than some
of them; he never made so much as an attempt to
write a strict fugue. But if he had 'learned' more,
if he had been more richly talented, he would presumably have become no more than a second Hasse
or a second Piccinni. And he would be as dead as
Hasse and Piccinni are today. What makes him
great is his mighty personality, his courage to 'say
the last thing.' He would have had the courage to
have Eurydice sent back to Hades, to have Orfeo
torn to bits by the Mænades, if the convention of
the period and the Viennese court had not insisted
on a 'happy end.' He did have the courage to write
the scene of the Furies in *Orfeo* and another in
Iphigénie en Tauride. He had the dramatic power,
the power of tragedy which the 'conciliatory' Goethe
lacked, according to his own confession. To grasp
the truth of this, one need only compare Goethe's
Iphigenia in Tauris, a magnificent humanistic work,
with the 'barbaric' version of Gluck.

While Gluck is not 'dead' (he stands, as it were,

in the glory of genuine greatness on credit), he is
not really alive; and this is due to the fact that he
worked exclusively in opera, which in any case is
the shortest-lived, most time-bound of all musical
species. Opera has the highest mortality rate: most
members of its genus, indeed, die immediately after
birth. Nor were they originally intended for a
lengthy career. The opera was always a festival
play; at best it was repeated a few times, either *in
situ* or at some neighboring princely courts. Later
on, it was not required to live longer than the duration of a short carnival or some other *stagione*.
Gluck, however, is the first whose works, although
written expressly for certain singers, no longer absolutely depend on certain singers. Indeed, his works
could be transplanted from the Italian stage to the
French and to the German. His music is the first
to be *bound up* with the libretto which was written
for him and no other composer. Metastasio wrote
'ideal' librettos, for the *opera seria* and the oratorio,
each of them set to music by twenty different composers. There is a 'Didone abbandonata' by Hasse,
Jommelli, Terradellas, Anfossi, Paesiello, Galuppi,
Maio, Manna, Sarti, Traetta, Vinci, and a dozen
others. But *the* 'Orfeo,' *the* 'Iphigenias,' and *the*

'Alceste' are the Orpheus, the Iphigenias and the Alceste of Gluck. And we have a definite feeling that even though Gluck may some day become a mere historical celebrity, like Dufay or Josquin, he is and remains great.

If Gluck's greatness may be 'suspect'; if it may be questioned—then the reader will think to himself, or openly, that the greatness of every musician of the nineteenth century after Beethoven and Schubert may be questioned, be his name Berlioz or Schumann, Wagner or Liszt, Brahms or Bruckner, Rossini or Verdi. To me it seems that the owners of three of these names have really become victims of the nineteenth century—Berlioz, Schumann, and Liszt. They were great, but not great enough. The nineteenth century, much abused, is truly the heroic age of the intellect—a century in which every creative man became a warrior, a fighter for the ownership of a tremendous heritage, for the worthy continuation of a too-powerful past. The heritage in the art of poetry was—let us say—Shakespeare and Milton, Racine and Voltaire, Lessing and Goethe. 'Romanticism' in England, France, and Germany may, among other things, be interpreted as a flight from the great responsibility, as a refusal to enter into the heritage. In music, Beethoven was the stumbling block. He was still a classicist; that is, he was born during music's age of innocence; but in many of his works, in the 'programmatic' sonatas and the symphonies, he could already be understood—and misunderstood—as a romanticist. The world was conscious of his overpowering greatness; once he was there, it was no longer possible to create at random, in a naive sort of way. His gigantic shadow was always in the background. Added to that was the new position of the musician, who was no longer a *Musikant*—a musical craftsman. Haydn had no 'higher education,' and didn't need it. What Mozart and Beethoven had in the way of education they had picked up, as it were, by intuition. Weber is a fateful figure in music, not least because he was the first 'educated musician' in Germany. Since Weber, there is hardly a musician of the nineteenth century who has not expressed himself in writing, as a poet or essayist, or as a critic, or at least as a writer of letters. The creative act, which always sways between the unconscious and the conscious, becomes ever more dependent, ever more weighty. One might classify musicians according to the degree to which they succeed in overcoming their consciousness, or in achieving a balance between the conscious and the unconscious.

∘ 8 ∘

It was especially difficult for Schumann. He was weighted down by a literary inheritance, as the son of a bookseller and a highly educated mother. It would have been easy for him, with his great talents, to have become a follower of his idol among the poets, Jean Paul Friedrich Richter, whose tangled romances, saturated with hyper-sentimentality, full of sublime flashes of imagination, but bare of all form, were the horror of the classicists, and whose shrinking band of readers are still divided into violent enthusiasts and violent rejectors. Schumann is absolutely unthinkable without these literary or poetic emotional stimuli. Behind nearly every one of his instrumental works there stands Jean Paul; he 'transposes' Jean Paul into music. Thus he came late to music and, except for his piano style, never fully mastered his craft. Even his richly inventive, enchanting piano style has a background of misfortune—the misfortune of the frustrated virtuoso who irreparably injured his hand by an excess of convulsive practising at his technique.

The same convulsiveness is present in Schumann's creative activity. His greatest moments are in the early works, in which he does not leave the pianistic battlefield: he has written nothing more original, more ravishing, more youthfully inspired than the 'Carnaval,' opus 9, or the 'Scenes of Childhood,' opus 15, or the Phantasy, opus 17 (dedicated to Liszt), or the 'Kreisleriana,' opus 16. The C-major Phantasy, for all its soaring flight, is somewhat weaker than the *scènes mignonnes* of the other works; and it is significant that the nearer he ventures into the vicinity of Beethoven the more he gets away from his own particular originality—which is his real greatness. This happens in the 'Grandes Sonates,' opus 11 and opus 14, and in the second sonata, opus 22. Later on, Schumann, the piano composer, becomes Schumann, the quartettist and symphonist, the composer of an opera and large choral works, and here the shadow of Beethoven must have grown ever higher and more threatening to his consciousness. Only as a song-writer is he happy, that is, in the early period: statistics would prove that all the *Lieder* which are immortal are on the low side of opus 50. It is the weight of the towering heritage that weighed on Schumann's creativeness—his consciousness, his critical intelligence. Schumann was forty-four years old (a dangerous age even for men—with feminine natures), when his mind, long overstrained, could no longer carry the load.

° 9 °

ANOTHER tragic case is that of Hector Berlioz. The son of the doctor of the Côte St. André, and himself, despite his music-madness, far too-long preoccupied with medical studies, was in every detail the opposite of Mendelssohn. It is quite natural that these two contemporaries should not only misunderstand each other, but detest each other, although they went for joint walking tours in the Roman Campagna. Mendelssohn had long finished a few of his most perfect works when Berlioz, at the age of twenty-three, finally and completely went over to music. Berlioz's autobiography, it is true, tells us how much he had composed from his earliest youth; but it tells us, too, how all this was but the expression of an irrepressible urge, without the support of competent and solid craftsmanship, which Mendelssohn never lacked, even in his earliest attempts. The one thing he is always certain of is his sincerity of feeling. Berlioz knows that passion is already as strongly developed in the child as in the youth and the man; and with him this passion propagates, even at the earliest age, the melodies (Berlioz says 'melody') of a romanza which he uses literally in the *largo* introduction to the Allegro of the *Symphonie Fantastique*. It is an exhibitionistic display of his feelings, endurable only because of Berlioz's nobility of soul. The Romanza itself was destroyed by Berlioz, together with the rest of his youthful attempts in chamber music. Mendelssohn never needed to destroy anything; whatever he produced always had form—*was* form. What Mendelssohn said about the clarity and definiteness of absolute music is exactly the opposite of the esthetic *credo* of Berlioz. To Berlioz, music was not exactly a means of clothing 'literary' objects or reminiscences in sound (that was reserved for Liszt, and Liszt's naive successor, Richard Strauss), but a medium through which to express impassioned or picturesque conceptions—preferably conceptions which are impassioned and picturesque at the same time. Or those which are the extreme opposite from the impassioned, such as the idyllic and simple in the *Enfance du Christ,* which is at the same time an opposite to another tendency of Berlioz, namely his liking of the colossal, his delight in hearing 24 horns perform the Andante in the *Freischütz* overture, or 36 double basses play their 'solo' in Beethoven's *Fifth Symphony.* This Don Quixote of music, as amiable and sometimes as tragi-comical as his literary prototype, lived as a musician in an imaginary world (as a man he was obliged to live all-too-much in Paris). And what a singular world it is! It is Virgil's *'Æneid,'* even more real to the southern Frenchman than to the direct descendants of Æneas, Ascanius and Romulus, for he is more Latin than all of them; it is the Orient tinted with melancholy and the romantic brigand world of Byron, the swashbuckling renaissance of Cellini—a reminiscence of Rome; it is Faust—not by Goethe but by some anti-Goethe; and above all it is Shakespeare, filtered through a Latin and romantic temperament. But Berlioz never saw what Verdi saw (and we shall prove it by documents), namely that behind all the musical media there is still something else—music itself. Just as behind the subject of every painting there is something different—the art of painting. Delacroix is greater than Berlioz. That is what makes musicians disagree so in their judgment of Berlioz: one group feels in his music, behind his music, the glowing, magnificent man who hated all that was Parisian, who never in his life or in his art wore a costume or a mask, who saw things through a distorting mirror only because of his overheated imagination and his lack of taste; the others see and feel only the shortcomings in his music. Whoever has heard several more or less equally good performances of the *Symphonie Fantastique,* which contains the whole Berlioz, is torn between two impressions. At one time he is swept away by the youthful sincerity of the 'Dreams and Passions,' and the dream-like objectivity of the 'March to the Scaffold'; and the next time everything appears to be empty, childish —merely 'descriptive music,' which means non-music.

There was descriptive music in earlier centuries, too. We possess a dozen different musical descriptions of a 'march to the scaffold,' namely Marie Antoinette's journey of death, set to music in a whole series of piano pieces between 1793 and 1803, which was the year of Berlioz's birth. But they are naive and inoffensive. Certainly Bach's Capriccio *'sopra la lontananza del suo fratello dilettissimo'* can in no way be compared with the slow movement of the *Symphonie Fantastique.* Berlioz, whose musical domestic idols were by no means Bach and Mozart and Haydn, but such already somewhat 'suspect' masters as Gluck, Weber and—Spontini, is one of the typical victims of the nineteenth century.

o 10 o

STILL another victim is Liszt. We are not referring to the present fate of Liszt's music, a fate sadder than that of the music of any other celebrated composer of the nineteenth century. We have been re-reading Wagner's article (or open letter to Marie Wittgenstein) on the symphonic poems of Franz Liszt. It begins with the writer's confession of his inability to say what is proper and essential; it then speaks of the virtuoso Liszt, crediting his performance of Beethoven's sonatas with the character, not of reproductions but creations (as though Liszt had something better, or at least different, to give than Beethoven); and closes with an appeal for confidence in Liszt, since he was not only the most musical of all musicians but much too noble a person to mislead or distress the listener. The quintessence of the article is a statement that the solution of the problem of the symphonic poem (at which Beethoven, for instance, had failed in his third 'Leonore' overture) 'could be reserved only for one of the most highly gifted among the elect—one who was not only through and through the perfect musician but through and through the contemplative poet.' Well, of the twelve or fourteen Liszt symphonic poems hardly one is still alive today, nor are his *Christus, St. Elizabeth,* the psalms, and the masses. Even of Liszt's piano works but few have survived, and least of all the most exacting and extensive of them, the B minor sonata.

Where does the fault lie? Certainly not in Liszt's so-called 'internationalism.' Orlando Lasso's internationalism did not prevent him from becoming one of the greatest Italian and at the same time French musicians of his time. The alleged Germanism of Gluck did not prevent him from becoming, successively, a very great Italian and a very great French composer of operas. If Ferruccio Busoni failed to become one of the world's great creators it was not because he was half Italian and half German, but just because he was Busoni, and therefore unable to reconcile the contradiction within himself, which was—to put it briefly—a contradiction between the heritage of Liszt on the one hand, and that of Mozart and Bach on the other. Liszt, of German extraction, but adopted by the Hungarians, was a Frenchman in education and feeling—or, more exactly, a Parisian, just as his daughter, Cosima, was a Parisian. There are, it is true, some very eminent Parisian musicians; for instance Claude Debussy, about whom Wagner would not have spoken as favorably as about Liszt. As a personality Liszt resembles most nearly a certain great German poet— in reality a Frenchman who wrote in German because he happened to be born in Swabia—namely Friedrich Schiller. It is not without reason that the République Francaise made Schiller one of its *citoyens,* while purposely omitting to do as much for Goethe. His dialectics, his sweep of sentiment, his revolutionary feeling, his rhetoric—all these attributes of Schiller's are French. Schiller is the German precursor of Victor Hugo.

Rhetoric—that's it. Rhetoric is not permitted in music. Liszt has used Bach for rhetorical purposes; but between rhetoric and expression there is an unbridgeable gap. To appreciate the difference, one need only compare Liszt's B-minor sonata with a sonata of Beethoven's, such as the Appassionata or the C-minor sonata, opus 111; with one of Schumann's or his C-major Phantasy; or with a sonata of Chopin's. Rhetoric, too, can be genuine, and it is more suitable for tempting the public than simple expression; but for a musical category it is inadequate; and in the long run it becomes impossible, because it is so easily discovered to be a sham. However, genuine expression is not incompatible with virtuosity. Chopin's music has great virtuoso qualities, but it is rarely rhetorical—only when he wanted it to be. Liszt was rhetorical because he could not be otherwise. Where he wants to be simple, he is affected. To Liszt, virtuosity was a danger. Only near the close of his life and his creative work, in some of his songs, do virtuosity and rhetoric fall away; and the simplicity of these pieces is very touching. But it is a negative simplicity—an absence of the objectionable; not the simplicity of strength and concentration.

Wagner's phrase to the effect that in Liszt the absolutely perfect musician and the absolutely contemplative poet had been fused is only a polite, diplomatic phrase. It is more nearly true to say that this musician-born-after-his-time, this virtuoso, this Beethoven-worshipper, takes refuge behind poetic design, in the manner of Berlioz—and yet very differently. With Liszt the 'program' is a vehicle for the music, very tasteful—as becomes a Parisian—and with a very subtle interweaving of themes—as becomes a musician so well educated psychologically, and so sophisticated. Only—none of these works was really finished. They lack the craftsmanship which Wagner commanded in such high and ever-increasing degree. A *grandseigneur* of music has sketched them out. They are fixed; but they might have been fixed in twenty different forms or variants. Liszt is the extreme opposite to Beethoven, who never fixed anything until it was completed. Liszt never completed anything, not even the invention of his motives. What Wagner praised in Liszt's symphonic poems, the 'inspired sureness of musical conception' ('*geniale Sicherheit der musicalischen Conception*') is the exact opposite of the truth. Liszt's beloved and friend, the Princess Carolyne Sayn-Wittgenstein, showed a much keener perception when she reproved him for leaving the instrumentation of his orchestral works to various assistants. Her letter (quoted from Peter Raabe's monograph on Liszt, II.78 f.) is so perspicacious that it may be considered an intuitive criticism of Liszt's essential shortcoming:

Why on earth do you entrust Raff with the orchestration of your Goethe-Marsch? What painter would be satisfied to deliver his pencil sketch and leave the coloring to a paint-mixer? Raff, you will say, is no mere paint-mixer. But he is not you! Instrumentation, too, depends on one's individuality, and his individuality is clumsy . . . It seems to me that you do not care enough about the coloring of your musical thoughts. You limit yourself to retouching. It seems to me that this is certainly not enough. And I compare it with style in literature: one never revises as one writes; one only invents according to the conditions which give one's thoughts their first form, their first formulation in words. A projected outline seizes the imagination, which perceives, as it were, a staked-out path ahead, but it discovers no new tracks, no new turns which might round out new variants of the thought one wants to express. I may be saying something stupid, but it seems to me that the style of this garment, the coloring of this thought, to which—quite rightly—you give such importance, always suffers if it has been traced, outlined and—

as it were—given, by another brain than that of the creator. I, at least, if I had this genius (no matter how impatient I might be) would much sooner allow others to do the filing, varnishing, shortening and polishing, than to permit the model of my design to be outlined. It would be impossible to me to follow other lines than my own; in order to kindle the sacred fire, these lines would have to be originally designed and dictated by my own mind.

Owing to this shortcoming Liszt, again, is the extreme antithesis to his younger contemporary, Johannes Brahms, the veritable musical goldsmith of the nineteenth century; but also to Wagner, who watched so fanatically over the careful execution of the smallest detail in his works—exactly because, from the first sketch to the last filing, every note was his own, and none was *improvised*. Liszt's symphonic and large choral works are improvisations on the grand scale, that is, edifices which are faulty or careless in their construction and a little too 'decorative' in their execution. But in the dome of St. Peter's the construction is both firm and esthetically pure; none of the decoration is extraneous, and each has its constructive meaning. And improvisation in the nineteenth century is no longer permitted.

(78)

Handel, in the eighteenth, was a great improvisor in his concertos and oratorios (contrary to Bach, who did not leave the smallest thing to chance); but his constructions were solid, and he knew that the decoration was in good hands. There were, in the course of the centuries, two great masters who liked to preserve the character, or the illusion, of improvisation, while in reality they calculated and determined even the smallest *fioriture,* namely Frescobaldi in the seventeenth and Chopin in the nineteenth century. In this point these two are antitheses to Liszt. Frescobaldi's solicitude is doubly astonishing for a period which saw in fantastic improvisations the apex of the virtuoso's art. With Chopin the illusion of improvisation is part of the fragrance of his art, so impassioned and tender, which can so easily be ruined by any clumsy handling; it is a kind of protection. Chopin had learned at the Grand Opéra, in Rossini and Bellini and Meyerbeer, what sort of *fioritura* brings out the applause, and he wanted to avoid that kind.

◦ II ◦

ONE cannot be a *grandseigneur* in music, in the sense that the composer Liszt was a *grandseigneur;* one must have mastered the craft down to the minutest and least-important twist. We are reminded, by the way, of the curious fact that all great musicians, as well as the majority of the great painters and sculptors (whose art, of course, necessarily partakes of craftsmanship) were very far from having an aristocratic ancestry. In the time of the Renaissance there were a few composer-princes, occasionally even some who composed professionally: Pope Leo X, Henry VIII, Duke Guglielmo Gonzaga, and Prince Carlo Gesualdo da Venosa. Yes, even the Hapsburgs, 'Roman Emperors of the German Nation,' composed quite decently through three generations. But Bach sprang from a musical artisan's family, a family of organists and town pipers; and Handel was the son of a barber-surgeon. Gluck was born in a forester's hut, Haydn in the poor hovel of a waggoner. Mozart and Beethoven again had musicians for fathers—Mozart a very ambitious, Beethoven a very unambitious one. Wagner, whether he was the son of the registrar Wagner or of the comedian Geyer, belonged to the small Saxon bourgeoisie; and the cottage at Le Roncole in which Giuseppe Verdi was born as the son of a poor *bottegaio* competes in wretchedness with the birthplace of Haydn. The only 'von' as prefix to the name of a musician, that of Carl Maria 'von' Weber has recently gone up in smoke; it was merely an arbitrary invention of Weber's father, who was a fraudulent braggard. Weber was so fortunate as to have inherited only a little of his character from his father, but all the more from his mother, a peasant's daughter, and his grandmother, the daughter of a Breton *chirurgus* and wig-maker. It is clear, things are very different in the field of music from the field of poetry, in which the aristocracy has accomplished so much that is praiseworthy. Great musicians come from the peasantry and the middle class; it was one of the little weaknesses of Beethoven that he deluded himself into believing he was of aristocratic lineage. In accordance with the law governing the preparation of great talent in the preceding generation, the sons of musicians, like Bach, Mozart and Beethoven, have an easier time; they 'arrive' and develop earlier than the musicians who lack such a heritage. For that reason Haydn and Verdi had great difficulties and developed comparatively late into what they really were. Later examples and counter-examples (without reference to their stature) are Richard Strauss and Busoni on the one side, and Anton Bruckner, the slow one, on the other. But one cannot establish a rule, as we see from the examples of Handel and Schubert.

o 12 o

ARE we unjust to Weber, Mendelssohn, Schumann, Berlioz, and Liszt? We are far from meaning to depreciate or 'criticize' them. Every celebrity of the nineteenth century, the century of consciousness, is 'suspect'—to repeat the expression—and none of the undisputed great ones, neither Wagner nor Verdi, neither Chopin nor Brahms, nor any of the more nationally limited representatives of nineteenth-century greatness, has been able to escape skeptical judgment. Wherever any of these 'undisputed' ones is great, he is doubly great; and wherever one of the 'disputed' ones is less great, it is to be charged not so much to his account as to the account of the century—the late century with the enormous heritage, with the all-too-lengthy memory. Of the three names—Wagner, Verdi, Brahms—the first two are usually found as opposites to the last, although the constellation is rather odd: one may well establish a relationship Wagner-Brahms, or a relationship Wagner-Verdi, but never a relationship Verdi-Brahms.

But is the relationship between Wagner and Verdi really valid? Does it go beyond the bare statement of fact that both were determined men of will, and both wrote operas and almost only operas? One in the north, the other in the south: the influence of both was international; indeed, each had an influence on the other's country, although Verdi fought the influence of Wagner in Italy with the greatest violence. But it is the most natural thing in the world that no Verdian can be a Wagnerian, and vice versa, if they are musicians and not just naive opera-goers. For Wagner himself, Verdi absolutely did not exist. Once they made contact with each other on the same field of action: when Wagner, a young man of twenty-two or twenty-three, committed the 'crime of his youth,' by writing his *Liebesverbot,* an opera based on Shakespeare's *Measure for Measure.* But at the age of twenty-four

Wagner already had finished with Shakespeare as a source of material, while Verdi was fascinated by Shakespeare for the rest of his life. What could a Verdi score have offered to Wagner—even *Otello* or *Falstaff*—if he could have lived to see them? He would have smiled over this *melodista,* this inventor of stereotyped impassioned melodies with primitive orchestral accompaniment. Whereas every page of his own scores, even where they look simple, is a symbol—an expression not only of his myriad-tongued orchestra, but the chasm-like depth of his thoughts and feelings. Not only to Wagner, but also to Friedrich Nietzsche, Wagner's brilliantly speculative admirer and hater, Verdi was a *quantité négligeable.* In Nietzsche's Bayreuth panegyrics, the *Untimely Observations,* there is not even a *derogatory* word about Verdi, there is no word about him at all. Only in the letters of Peter Gast to Nietzsche (Peter Gast is the man whom Nietzsche mistook for a great musician) there occurs a single reference to the 'hurdy-gurdy nonsense of Verdi and others . . .' In his anti-Wagner writings, to be sure, Nietzsche thinks of Brahms as an anti-pope of Wagner, but not of Verdi. And Nietzsche's pæan of praise for Bizet's *Carmen* is admittedly a malicious joke.

Verdi, on the other hand, did not hate Wagner, for he was not so stupid as not to recognize Wagner's greatness, but he hated Wagner's influence on Italian music. He felt in Wagner's operas the dominance of Germany's instrumental heritage, which he regarded as pernicious. He himself wrote a string quartet, but he cursed the composing of Italian quartets, symphonies, and symphonic poems. And it is only a logical consequence if the younger generation of Italian musicians, who see in Italy's exclusive cultivation of opera a danger for the future, hate Verdi as thoroughly as Verdi would have ignored them.

But Verdi is beyond doubt, and by right occupies a place beside Wagner, despite his primitive qualities, despite his esthetics. His true esthetics are, of course, to be deduced entirely from his works; but a little, too, from his letters—this inexhaustible, yet all-too-neglected source of information concerning his personality. The letters are full of contradictions. 'Verdi's Esthetics': a study bearing this title would have aroused his deepest rage, deeper even than his anger over the publication of his letters, or the attempt to gain an insight into his private life, which

attempt he always combatted most fiercely as a rude
violation of his personal rights. Only his work concerned the public, nothing else. And his work is
devoid of any autobiographical purpose, such as
may be detected, for instance, in Wagner's *Meistersinger,* or still more in that conceited, lamenting—
and lamentable—piece of dramatic exhibitionism by
a more recent 'German master,' namely Hans Pfitz-
ner's *Palestrina.* Verdi, unlike Wagner, had no desire to explain himself, to give reasons for his work
by means of words, to justify it or support it. We
shall get to know the deeper reasons for this later
on. He needed no supporting evidence. Whenever,
in his letters, a musical or artistic avowal escapes
him, he always seeks to soften it down at the end,
or to negate it: 'What tiresome chatter! What useless inanities!' It is impossible to fancy Verdi as a
writer of memoirs, like Berlioz or Wagner. He was
neither sentimental nor conceited enough.

Verdi's esthetics—this does not mean the drama-
turgy of Verdi's operas, which one might adduce
and formulate from his correspondence with his
librettist. That is a chapter in itself, which has to
do only indirectly with the question of Verdi's
greatness. It would show that Verdi, as in all things

concerning life and art, knew exactly what he wanted, and that in a certain sense he not only selected his own subjects just as much as Wagner did, but also formulated his own libretti. In *Aida* this act of formulation even includes versification. He knew exactly wherein his greatness as an opera composer consisted; this one may gather—not, of course, from observations about himself (that sort of thing does not exist with him) but from a few rare and brief critical remarks concerning others; for instance about Charles Gounod (who for him does not count as a dramatist) or concerning the *Mefistofele* of his friend Boito, whose weaknesses he bares without pity—all friendship notwithstanding.

Once Verdi expressed himself publicly, or semi-publicly, concerning esthetic matters; or at least he had to consider that his remarks would become publicly known. That was in January 1871, when he refused a call to become Mercadante's successor as head of the Naples Conservatory. He did this in a letter which ends with a maxim that was to become famous: *'Torniamo all'antico: sarà un progresso'*—'Let us return to the old: it will be an advance.' Verdi formulated the principles which he would have tried to maintain as the head of such an institution as follows:

I would have supported myself, so to speak, with one foot on the past and with the other on the present and future (for I am not at all afraid of the 'music of the future'). I would have said to the young pupils: train yourselves also in counterpoint, consistently, perseveringly to the last and until your hand masters the notes with freedom and firmness, according to your will. Thus you will learn to compose with sureness, to lead your voices well, to modulate without forcing. Study Palestrina and some few of his contemporaries. Then make a jump to Marcello, paying particular attention to his recitatives. Listen only to few modern operas, and don't be tempted by their numerous harmonic and orchestral charms, nor by the chord of the diminished seventh, the rock and refuge of all of us who cannot compose a bar without a half dozen of such sevenths . . .

He demands, besides, an extensive literary education; he warns against adding new recruits to the band of imitators and those who are suffering from the 'sickness of our time.'

Is this Verdi? No, this is an old reactionary professor, something like the caricature of Cherubini which Berlioz has left us. He says things which are self-understood or not to be understood; he says things which are beneath his dignity. Most incomprehensible of all is the 'historical program' which this homily contains. True, it would have been like Verdi to say: study the Italians, not the Germans; study vocal, not instrumental, music. But why Palestrina? To study Palestrina is easy; to understand him, very difficult. At any rate, his pedagogical value to the productive musician of today is effective only in the case of a master, not a pupil; and with the master only indirectly, by way of trans-substantiation. And why jump over the seventeenth century? Across Monteverdi, Frescobaldi, Carissimi, Steffani, Corelli? The seventeenth century is the real glory of Italian musical history. And why to Benedetto Marcello? Marcello, all in all, is a musician of the second or third rank, even in the recitatives of his 'psalms,' to which Verdi presumably refers. From sheer fear of publicity, for fear of being misunderstood, Verdi said precisely what cannot be understood.

Perhaps his manifesto can only be explained historically. He who has lived long in Italy finally acquires heretical opinions concerning Italian 'musicality' in the nineteenth and twentieth centuries. It is a barbaric musicality—partly uncouth, partly devoted to the pretty-pretty things which correspond to the familiar alabaster reproductions of the Tower of Pisa and the Moses of Michelangelo. Hence the return to Palestrina, whom Verdi names because he knew nothing about Frescobaldi and Carissimi. And he feared that the rest of musical Italianism, which in his early days he still found in Bellini and Donizetti, might be lost to the Italian musician, what with string quartets and symphonies and the like. What he meant by 'torniamo all'antico' we learn from *Falstaff*, the last *opera buffa* of the eighteenth and nineteenth centuries and the first of the twentieth. But of such things only the master is capable, not the pupil. And (we shall say more about this later) he must first become very old. Fundamentally, Verdi had quite different opinions about counterpoint. In April 1864 he heard someone say concerning Rossini's *Petite Messe solennelle* that Rossini had 'made progress,' had 'studied.' His comment was: 'Ugh! studied what? For his sake I would rather that he might unlearn music and write a second "Barbiere" . . .'

A letter to his friend Clarina Maffei (17 December 1884) reveals what Verdi really thought. He is against German music in general, and presumably against Wagner in particular. 'I am convinced,' he says, 'that this artificial art, peculiar even in its germ, is not adapted to our nature. We are positivists, and to a great extent skeptics. Our faith is weak, and in the long run we cannot believe in the fantastic capers of this foreign art, which lacks all naturalness and simplicity. And art without naturalness and simplicity is no longer art! The act of creation is necessarily based on the simple . . .' To Arrivabene he writes (12 February 1884): 'Good pieces of work always are, and have at all times been, rare; today they are almost non-existent . . . You ask why? Because there is too much music being made. Because too many experiments are being tried. Because people look into the darkness and don't see the sun. Because we have exaggerated the outlines. Because we want to make the monstrous instead of the great. And out of the monstrous grows the insignificant, and the *baroque*. That is the point at which we have arrived.'

He wants the great. Seriousness, with him, goes without saying. 'The great' is not the grand opera, a *genre* with which some people have tried to asso-

ciate Verdi's art—and not altogether without justification when one thinks of the *Sicilian Vespers* and
Don Carlos, and if one does not penetrate beyond
the externals. Indeed he did not despise Meyerbeer;
he simply did not understand him at all; he did
not care about him one way or the other. On 5 September 1847, he heard Halévy's *La Juive* in Paris
—and was inexpressibly bored. He esteemed Rossini,
but he kept his distance from him. 'What I desire
in art,' he says (29 July 1868) 'is not, what the
Olympian Jupiter of Passy [i.e. Rossini] wants—
merely pleasure.' Art is not entertainment. 'To have
been entertained! That is a phrase which even in
my youth drove the blood to my head, and which
still transports me into all states of fury.'

As we have mentioned before, music—true music
—is to him what lies *behind* the music, or works
behind the music. It is this conviction that most
frequently drives him, in later years, to make confessions, such as this:

Some would like to be melodists like Bellini, others, harmonists like Meyerbeer; I, neither the one nor the other.
And I wish that the young musician, when he sits down
to write, would forget about being a melodist or harmonist,

idealist, futurist or any other of the devilish things connected with all this pedantry. Melody and harmony must not be permitted to be anything but media in the artist's hands with which to make *music;* and if the day should ever come when people speak neither of melody nor harmony, neither of German nor Italian schools, neither of the past nor the future, etc.—then perhaps we shall enter the kingdom of art.

And again:

When it comes to musical confessions of faith, one must be generous, and I, for my part, am extremely tolerant. I respect the melodists, the harmonists, the bores and those who wish to be bored at all costs because it is a part of good manners. I respect the past and the present, and I would respect the future, if I knew it and found that it was good. In short, melody, harmony, declamation, fioritura, orchestral effects, local color—nothing but words which are often on our lips and which mostly just hide the absence of any sense. They are only means to an end. If with these means you make good music, I shall be content—with all kinds. In the 'Barbiere,' the phrase *'Signor, giudizio, per carità'* is neither melody nor harmony; but it is the correct and true expression of the word—it is *music* . . . Amen.

(Verdi does not quote quite exactly; he means the passage in the trio of Act I, when Rosina recognizes Count Almaviva behind the mask of the seemingly intoxicated blacksmith of the regiment.) Finally, at the time of *Aida* he says: 'Just don't be a melodist, exclusively a melodist, in music. There is something more in music than melody and harmony, namely music! You may find this puzzling. Well, neither Beethoven nor Palestrina were melodists. That is, melodists in our sense.'

But Verdi has the strictest opinions about the core of his creativeness, the characteristic melody born of situation and character. Coloratura he does not regard as melody. At one time (1871) Andrea Maffei, the husband of his friend, Clarina Maffei, offered him a translation of *Anacreon* to be set to music. He refused with these words: 'This is a type of poetry which does not accord with my feeling, and which does not seem to me suitable to be set to music—or rather which I am not suitable to set to music. I would not succeed in producing anything worth while, and neither Anacreon, nor you, nor I would gain anything by it.' Verdi was not the man to catch the spirit of *Anacreon*. At the same time he also refuesd to compose some verses by his friend, Arrivabene. 'Your verses are very nice, but I am not the man to compose Album Leaves or the like.' (Compare this with Liszt, the accommodating composer, among whose songs—Vol. III of the Complete Edition—we find settings of texts by Pohl, Wiegeleben, Bodenstedt, Scheffel, the Princess Hohenlohe, etc.) 'And do you think that I have written a melody when I have fixed up a few trills and an ascending run in imitation of the nightingale? I should like to emphasize that melodies do not consist of runs, trills and turns . . . Please note that melodies are, for instance, the Chorus of Bards (in Bellini's "Norma"), the Prayer in "Mosè" (Rossini) and so forth; but there is no melody in the cavatinas of "Barbiere," in the "Gazza ladra," the "Semiramide," and so on. What are they, then, you will ask. What you will, but certainly not melodies, and still less good music. Don't be angry if I debit one to Rossini, but he can stand it . . .' And further (16 April 1873): 'In the "Barbiere," except for *Ecco ridente in cielo* there is no melody at all . . . Solfeggio, yes, but not melody . . .'

What does Verdi mean? Does he not thus condemn some of his own pieces, such as the first aria of Leonora in *Trovatore,* the E-major aria of Gilda,

(95)

and half of Violetta's role in *Traviata?* Perhaps, presumably. We do know that he considered the last aria of Leonora in *Forza del destino,* the Queen's scene in *Don Carlos,* Rigoletto's duet and monologue in Act I, the love scene in *Ballo in maschera* (to name some earlier works), and the whole of *Aida* (to name the work which leads up to *Otello* and *Falstaff*) to be melody—his kind of melody. Two observations comprise all of Verdi's esthetics—the esthetics of the great Verdi. One dates from 1876, when he attended the performance of a naturalistic drama. His comment was: 'To copy what is true may be good. But to invent the true is better, much better. Maybe it will seem to you that there is a contradiction in the words "to invent the true"; but just ask father' (in Italian, *Papà,* as Verdi always calls Shakespeare). 'It is possible that he, *Papà,* knew a Falstaff, but hardly a villain so villainous as Iago, and never angels like Cordelia, Imogen, or Desdemona. And yet they are so *true!*' The other observation came ten years earlier, in connection with a mention of Manzoni's great novel: 'That is a truthful book, as true as truth itself. Oh, if only the artists would once grasp the truth—there would no longer be musicians of the future and of the past, neither puritan, realistic, and idealistic painters, nor classic and romantic poets—but only poets, painters, musicians.'

Verdi's greatness is very easy to sense, but very difficult to explain; it is not obvious. One mark of greatness he shares with Gluck, with Shakespeare, and all great dramatists: he is not conciliatory. Manrico, Leonora, Azucena must die a pitiless death: not even the music concedes to them and the listener a reconcilation in its ideal sphere, as it does to the dying in *Forza del destino,* in *Ballo in maschera,* and above all in *Aida.* Especially in his old age Verdi is without mercy and without illusions: the characters in *Falstaff* are all puppets in the hand of a god who for his own amusement allows them to wriggle a little—*'tutto nel mondo è burla.'* Poor Desdemona dies without musical glory; her death and that of Othello are as bitter as death itself. No 'apotheosis' like Isolde's *Liebestod,* Elizabeth's romantic—and, from a medical point of view, so mysterious—passing-away, or Brünnhilde's suicide in heroic equestrian pose.

As regards Verdi's musical greatness, the comparison with his Saxon antithesis is equally helpful. The difference between the two is not unlike the

difference between the themes of a fugue and a sonata. A sonata subject needs to be no more than a
germ, out of which something is developed. One
immediately thinks of Beethoven and his delight in
developing insignificant and often even worthless
motives into sublime things. The motives of the
Finales to the Trios opus 1, No. 3, or the violin
sonata opus 30, No. 2, are examples of such truly
worthless, provoking themes. It has been counted
a weakness in Schubert's piano sonatas that the full
and luscious melodiousness of the themes militate
against a really exciting working-out. Quite right:
a good sonata theme should be something less. A
fugue theme, on the contrary, is nothing if it is
not plastic, if it does not appear as a complete character on the scene. Never can a good fugue be developed from a poor subject. Reversing this statement,
a good fugue theme, if only it is treated correctly,
can never result in a bad fugue. Now I shall not
assert that Wagner's motives are insignificant, let
alone worthless; as dramatico-musical symbols they
are admirably plastic. But they are only the bricks
of a symphonic edifice; they have value only *as* symbols. Wagner is a great tactician; he wins his battles
after a hundred secret maneuvers. Verdi, on the

contrary, must conquer with the first attack, or the battle is lost. He must deliver his most powerful melodic strokes, and he does deliver them. Wagner works with time-bombs, the explosion follows only after an exactly calculated period. Verdi is an explosive musician from the beginning to the end.

° 13 °

THE common objections to calling Wagner great are based on other grounds, namely on Wagner the man. There are also objections to Wagner the artist, and pretty nearly all of them have been summed up by Nietzsche in his anti-Wagnerian pamphlets—indeed, so perfectly, with such infernal clairvoyance that later generations of Wagner enemies have been unable to add anything. He deals with Wagner's hostility to life; his effeminacy; the decadence, the physiological effect, the histrionics of his art. I shall not mention the insult aimed at Wagner by Busoni, the admirer of Bach and Mozart, in comparing him with Baccio Bandinelli. All that is true, yet it has nothing to do with Wagner's greatness. It separates him from masters like Bach and Handel, Mozart and Haydn, Beethoven and Schubert. Wagner belongs to quite another category of musicians—a sequence which begins with Carl Maria Weber. One simply could not make music in the nineteenth century as one did in the eighteenth. There could be no Michelangelos in the nineteenth century, much less Donatellos. Wagner—the later, the real Wagner—was no longer concerned with music, at least not with music alone. Where he wants to be effective as a pure musician, where he competes, so to speak, as a melodist with other opera composers (for instance, Meyerbeer) Wagner the great conqueror suffers some awful defeats. How many melodic horrors there are in the *Flying Dutchman* or in *Tannhäuser,* witness Eric's B-flat-major lament, 'Though all I have is thine forever' or the duet between Elizabeth and Tannhäuser, with Wolfram in the background as the resigned third—resigned, too, in a musical sense—a piece which in every respect is one of the darkest spots in Wagner's works. This sometimes embarrassing *'melodista'* has, however, little to do with the real, the great, Wagner, the Wagner who wants to conquer the *whole* man through his art, through poetry and music, who demands not only seeing and hearing, but abandonment to the last ventricle of one's heart. Whoever was, or is, not capable of such complete surrender, is and was an anti-Wagnerian from the start.

There have always been such anti-Wagnerians, such antagonists by instinct. And the antagonism has grown more and more as sources of information about the man Wagner became available, and as the Wagner legend created by Wagner himself and fostered by 'Bayreuth' was being replaced by objective truth. Wagner's case was exactly the reverse of Verdi's: Verdi's stature grew greater and greater, the more his letters and utterances became known; but when Wagner's autobiography was finally made available to the public, a profound shock went through the ranks of his adherents—in view of all this 'unadorned truth' which still concealed so much, and twisted so much more. I am, of course, aware of all the reasons and objections with which in all historical matters one may assail the idea of 'objective truth.' History is not a science in the strict sense. History is always 'giving meaning to the meaningless.' We never know all the evidence, and we always run the danger of interpreting falsely even that which we really know. We do this in fifty cases out of a hundred. And all biographical writing is even more questionable. We never know a person, his reasons and his background, completely. He may be an accomplished hypocrite, and that may be reflected in all his letters and remarks—especially since the nineteenth century, when even intimate letters begin to be written with a view—or at least a glance—to future publication. Doubt has been cast on the honesty even of Mozart's letters—letters which were never intended for the public, letters that are so transparent in every poor attempt to mislead the addressee just a little, say the writer's father, or his wife! In the opposite way the contradiction between the legend about Wagner the 'master' and Wagner the man might be resolved in Wagner's favor. In other words, no letter, no utterance of Wagner was made without an eye to posterity. Each was given a costume, a mask. We see through the mask, we know only too well the discrepancy between self-portrayal and truth, between mask and face. Nevertheless, one might want to prove that the face under the mask was not so bad.

That is difficult. It does happen sometimes that an overpowering talent falls to a detestable human being; there may be examples in literature or in painting. In Philosophy, Francis Bacon is the best-known example; but Bacon's doubtful morals do not detract from his intellectual discoveries. However, in music one cannot lie. Wagner was detestable as a man, and the histrionics which Nietzsche criticized in Wagner's art are histrionics in another, more dubious sense. Is that the trouble? And is the 'intelligible' Wagner better than the 'empirical' Wagner?

He is, really. He must be. There are in Wagner's life examples of moral turpitude that would seem unpardonable in any man, things which no biographer can hush up or gloss over, things which are not to be excused on the ground of the extraordinary qualities of the man, but which seem even more reprehensible because of them. It is quite true that extraordinary people cannot be measured by the moral yardstick of the middle class. So-called 'erotic' delinquencies may be ignored altogether. It is of no consequence whatever if Michelangelo had perverse sexual emotions; so had all the Greeks, for instance, at the time of Socrates and Plato. It matters not whether Tchaikovsky resembled Michelangelo—and so many other great painters and poets —in this respect: if only his music were sometimes cleaner. The question of Wagner's two marriages, too, is beside the point. Nobody has the right to

play the judge between Minna and Richard; nobody is called upon to pity poor Hans von Bülow
and to throw stones at Richard and Cosima; nobody
need look askance at the creator of *Parsifal* when he
tries to lighten the oppressive conjugal yoke of
Cosima (and it was sometimes more oppressive than
Minna's), nor when he gets his inspiration for the
figure of Kundry from the beauteous and full-
blooded Judith Gautier. No, the things that weigh
against Wagner are of another kind. The creator of
the character of the youthful hero who has 'never
learned fear' is also the revolutionary of 1848 who
observes the sanguinary events from the safe eleva-
tion of the tower of the Kreuzkirche in Dresden,
and consequently avoids capture and imprisonment,
but makes his escape after the enterprise has failed;
he is the man who so ardently desires his Parisian
success in 1861, and ten years later writes 'A Capit-
ulation'—the most miserable and incidentally hu-
morless slander that was ever perpetrated on a
defeated nation by one of the most outstanding representatives of the victorious country; the anonymous writer who circulates the pamphlet entitled
Judaism in Music, but at the same time writes the
most cringing letters to Giacomo Meyerbeer, the

mighty ruler of the Berlin Court Opera; the journal-
ist who derides Rossini, but—as the result of a half
hour's conversation with the *gran buffone*—writes
a benevolent obituary about him (*'de mortuis nil
nisi bonum'*); the debtor who gives his scores in
pawn to his most generous friend, Otto Wesendonck, but who, when the friend is no longer
needed, is mean enough to demand them back—
without further ado—for his 'royal benefactor.'

His relationship with this 'royal benefactor' is
probably the most serious charge against Wagner's
character: we are aware of it only since, a few years
ago, Bayreuth has had the herostraic courage to
publish his correspondence with Ludwig II *in ex-
tenso*. It is simply not possible to beat the unscrupu-
lousness with which Wagner exploited the poor
young king, who felt and understood only the most
elementary and material side of Wagner's art, and
who imbibed it just as addicts to alcohol and mor-
phine imbibe their poisons; and one cannot excuse
the unconscionable way with which he inflated him
into the roles of his heroes (Lohengrin, Stolzing,
Siegfried, Parsifal). Two people came together who
intellectually seemed to be predestined for one another: the artist who wished to substitute art for

life, and the ecstatic young man whose illness was flight from reality, and who, being a king, believed himself entitled to cultivate this disease. Wagner's champions have not attempted to prove that Wagner, with his understanding of people, did not recognize the mental disease of his victim at the first glance; they have been satisfied naively to deny the existence of this mental disease. The perverse disposition of the unhappy youth, which unconsciously played a part in this friendship from beginning to end, could, however, not be denied.

Wagner was unable to hold a single friend, without crises, to the end of his life; as a writer of polemics—against Hebbel, against Brahms—he fought with the most perfidious journalistic weapons; in his autobiography he took posthumous revenge on just about all his contemporaries. That is the soil in which grew the great works of art in which we are asked to believe. Just imagine Bach, Haydn, Mozart, Beethoven, Schubert, and ask yourself whether their art could have prospered on such moral foundations. If Wagner is great, his greatness is in any case a different one from that of his so-called predecessors, among whom, by the way, he really recognized only Beethoven; for what has 'the genius of light and love' that he saw in Mozart to do with the real Mozart? And how little even the real Beethoven has to do with the composer of the *Ninth Symphony,* the only Beethoven whom Wagner recognized!

All Wagner's 'mistakes,' all his unscrupulous acts, his insincerities, his shameless behavior, are explained by the fact that they were committed for the sake of his work. He knew that he had to create his own new world by struggling against 'the world'; every form of egotism seemed to him permissible, and was permissible for the *work.* Even the flight from Dresden after the abortive revolution, even the exploitation of an insane king. Personally Wagner was far beyond and above all patriotic ways of thinking; accordingly he also tried, later on, to get his son exempted from German military service and so save him from every possibility of a *'Heldentod'* (hero's death). But he himself was a hero undaunted from beginning to end—for his *work.* His best moment, his most warm-hearted behavior came after the Munich reverses of 1865, while previously, in the years of good fortune, he had behaved like a genuine parvenu. At a time when

so many musicians were so bourgeois, and worse—
namely philistines—he was an anti-philistine, much
more than Liszt, for all of Liszt's regal gypsydom.
The philistines have charged him with unscrupu-
lousness in money matters, with his alleged ex-
travagance and love of luxury. But he is quite right
when he says that the creation of a world out of
chaos could not have taken place in a garret. No one
has quarrelled with Beethoven for indulging exactly
the same tendency, when he got a few Viennese
aristocrats to guarantee his existence and the security behind which he might build up his esoteric
world. In a letter to Mathilde Wesendonck, of 3
October 1858 (a letter already quoted by Thomas
Mann in his beautiful essay on the 'Sufferings and
Greatness of Richard Wagner'), Wagner himself
formulated it beyond contradiction, emphasizing
the discrepancy between his 'empirical' and 'intelligible' personality:

What a hard life I have of it, to be sure! When I think
of the vast expenditure of care, worry and pain I need,
merely to procure myself a little leisure from time to time,
I'm inclined to be ashamed of going on imposing myself
in this way on existence, since the world, speaking strictly,

will really have nothing to do with me. Thus forever and ever to be fighting for provision of the needful, often obliged for whole long periods to think of absolutely nothing but how to set about obtaining outward quiet and the requisites of existence for a little time ahead; and for that to have so entirely to depart from my own way of feeling, to appear to those through whom I want myself maintained so altogether different from what I am,—it truly is revolting. And added to it all, to be framed the very way to recognize it as none other. All these cares come so naturally to a man who views life as an end in itself, who finds in concern for provision of the needful the best sources for his imaginary enjoyment of the finally procured. For which reason, also, no one else can quite understand why this is so absolutely repugnant to a man like me, seeing that it is the lot and condition of all men; that for once in a way a man should just not view life as an end in itself, but as an unavoidable means to a higher end—who will comprehend that right earnestly and clearly? *

In his fight and his suffering for his work Wagner is something more than an actor. And there are a thousand things in his work which are more than

* Excerpt of letter translated by William Ashton Ellis. Scribner's, New York, 1905.

histrionics. Wagner was not just the musical Makart of his century. About this we shall speak at length in another connection.

o 14 o

IN comparison with Wagner, Brahms seems like a philistine. The difference in character and clarity of vision becomes most apparent in their attitude towards the Reich after the German victory of 1871 —about which Verdi, for instance, also used some painful words. (For although Verdi did not like France, he hated Germany.) Wagner saw deeply enough to realize the hollowness, the futility of this victory, which changed and spoiled the German character. Whoever is familiar with the writings and letters of his last twelve years knows that there never was a more severe critic of this Bismarckian Reich, notwithstanding the *Kaisermarsch*, his most bombastic composition. In this point he was in full agreement—in sentiment, if not in thought—with Friedrich Nietzsche. Brahms, too, has paid his tribute to the German victory with a mediocre composition, his *Song of Triumph*, on which Wagner commented so maliciously—this time with justification. (The value of patriotic compositions is mostly in inverse ratio to its success—witness Beethoven's *Battle of Vittoria*.) And Brahms, born in a Free City of the Reich, has never gone beyond this patriotic point of view of a philistine; he spared himself all deeper criticism of the Reich and its potentates and citizens. When his Swiss friend, Joseph Victor Widmann, inveighed against the young Kaiser's 'sporting' remark that forty million Germans would sooner 'die in their tracks' than return a single stone of Alsace-Lorraine, Brahms administered an indignant rebuke to Widmann, and never quite got over his resentment. How right Widmann has proved to be! How lacking in freedom was Brahms! And, on the other hand, how unconventional was his relationship with Clara Schumann, who was destined to be the cause of so many disappointments! And how heroic was Brahms's life—in a wholly different sense from Wagner's!

The problem of the greatness of Johannes Brahms lies in the fact that he was no revolutionary like Wagner, but a late-comer, a man born after his time—and that he knew it. He knew that he came late, and perhaps too late. His greatness lies in his having mastered this situation, and in the way he mastered it. He did not try, like Liszt (who is really one of his antitheses) to get around the heritage of the past— around Beethoven, Mozart, and Haydn, around Bach and Schubert. The respective relationships of Liszt and Brahms to Schubert are very characteristic. Liszt regarded Schubert—more exactly, Schubert's *Lied*—rather like a wild flower which one uses for a button-hole, because of its fragrance and charm. Brahms, however, has a deep feeling for the sounds of nature that vibrate in Schubert's melodies, for his harmonic discoveries and splendors, for his South German open-heartedness and his gay colors, which must have been especially coveted by him— the shy and taciturn German of the north. Brahms remained a North German composer, yet he became a Viennese. On this path of development, or transformation, he took many a false step. Taciturnity and reserve are often compensated for by sentimentality; and Brahms at times is one of the most sentimental of composers, witness the first movement of the B-flat-major piano concerto! Schubert is never sentimental, because he is able to speak out freely, from the fullness of his heart.

Brahms did not fight shy of Schubert; nor did he avoid Mozart, Bach, and above all Beethoven. How easy it was for Wagner, the opera composer and revolutionary, for whom only the *Ninth Symphony* existed out of Beethoven's total work—and perhaps the late string quartets; and how difficult for Brahms, the symphonist and composer of sonatas and other chamber music of all sorts, for whom Beethoven was a stumbling block at every turn! But he was brave and accepted the entire past. He reckoned that the listener, too, knows and understands the past. The listener, too, is a late-comer. When it was suggested to him—to Brahms—that the principal motive of the Finale of the C-minor symphony resembled the Hymn of Joy in the *Ninth Symphony* he answered that every donkey could notice it. Indeed, it not only resembles the Hymn of Joy theme; it is consciously modelled after it. And Brahms's work is not weakened by its relation to the great art of the past: it is strengthened by it. Just as a piece of sculpture by Michelangelo, or a picture by Titian is not weakened, but strengthened, by its relation to—not imitation of—the works of antiquity. Just as Goethe's most beautiful poems, those of the *West-östliche Divan,* derive strength from their relation to Persian poetic art.

Brahms's music is always related to something.

There is so much in the musical past that he loved
—folksongs, sixteenth-century a-cappella music,
Bach and Handel, Haydn and Mozart, and, after
his youthful love for Schumann and Chopin, the
works of the more and more distant past, besides
Beethoven, whom he never forgot. His is an art of
living memories; its relations to the past are effective at every turn. Wagner, in the *Meistersinger,*
is able to contrast his own personal style with a style
of a previous age, and so to deride his own work and
applaud it at the same time. Brahms is not capable
of this. He feels himself to be the late, last musician
of a great, a super-great, tradition which he never
forgets or denies. His art must necessarily be an expression of love and surrender, but also of pessimism
and resignation. He has donned many masks, including that of the naive person, the out-and-out
Teuton, the Hungarian; but the finish is resignation—in the form of chamber music with clarinet
and the 'Four Serious Songs.' Anything simpler
and more definitive cannot be said than has been
expressed in these works. Brahms is not an imitator
but a living epilogue. As such he is great. He was
the last post-classical composer. He had mastered
the heritage of the past. (We shall have to return

to this in the historical part of this book.) The men who came after his death, however, were *obliged* to destroy this heritage, because they could not master it.

At the end of his life and work Wagner does the same as Brahms: he writes 'related' music; he merges his personal style with the style of the past. Why did Wagner decide not to set the Buddhistic drama, *The Victors,* to music, and why did he prefer Parsifal, which one might call a romantic-medieval variant of the ancient Indian subject, or—as a Schopenhauer disciple might say—an 'incarnation' of this unborn opera's 'will'? Because for *The Victors* he would have had to create a new melodic idiom, as he had done in the case of *Tristan*. And presumably because, thanks to his intuitive artistic sagacity, he realized that an 'oriental' stimulus would not have been productive in connection with his style. Therefore he chose and used the Roman Catholic, the Gregorian, the Palestrinian *milieu*. He, too, becomes a beneficiary of the past. It *was* a way of making things easier; it was even in some measure an exploitation—most distinctly so at that incredible moment when Titurel's voice resounds three times through the vaulted nave—unaccompanied, like a priest at the altar; when the silence of an immense and ancient sanctuary suddenly begins to speak. This is something quite different from the exploitation of the pre-classical, baroque musical style in the *Meistersinger*. Here, in *Parsifal*, Gregorian chant and the influence of old a-cappella music is fused with Wagner's personal speech, and all opposing elements are resolved. And *Parsifal* is not weaker but stronger for it, just as Brahms's music has not been weakened but strengthened by absorbing so many ingredients from the musical past.

III

Esoteric Conditions for Greatness

We begin life in a state of dwarfishness, incoherence, and
perplexity. Greatness is what lies beyond us.
BURCKHARDT, *Observations on World History.*

*A*S we survey the various series of volumes which make up the Complete Editions of the Masters, we see that in each case they are very large: 33 volumes of Palestrina, and many more of Lasso; 17 of Schütz—comparatively few for so long a life—but all the more of the short-lived Purcell; 46 Annual Series of Bach and twice as many of Handel. There are two astonishing series of Mozart and Schubert, both of whom died young; and impressively long ones of Beethoven, Schubert, Mendelssohn, and Berlioz. The justification for these long series has often been questioned, for instance by Brahms. True, Brahms was himself a member of the committee for the publication of Bach's works, and let none of the newly appearing volumes pass without notice; but he was of the opinion that it would suffice if manuscript copies of all the less important works, all those of merely 'philological' interest, could be deposited for reference purposes in some of the large libraries. He was quite right—for his own time, which was in any case not an Alexandrian era, and which knew no wars with so highly developed a technique of destruction as our own.

However, what is 'merely philological'? Is Beethoven's 'Duet for two obbligato eye-glasses'—a little masterpiece of humor—less masterly for being almost unknown? The knowledge of Schubert songs among the common run of singers is mostly limited to about five dozen—namely those contained in the ready-made selections which are set out for them by a handful of editors employed by certain publishers. These, in turn, are influenced by the traditional mental laziness of our sopranos, contraltos, tenors, and basses. But it is one of the greatest experiences in the life of a real musician to embark —all alone—on a voyage of discovery in the ten volumes of *Lieder* in the Schubert Complete Edition. Four Mozart symphonies are included in the repertoire of our conductors—and they are there by right; yet the two 'little' symphonies in A major and G minor (Koechel Nos. 201 and 183) are inferior to them only in size, not in mastery. And what is true of Schubert songs is true of Haydn's quartets and Haydn's symphonies.

There are some music critics writing in Sunday supplements who lament, with remarkable judicial discernment, the productivity of the great masters. According to these writers, the masters wrote much too much, and too much that is inconsequential or even worthless. But productivity is an integral part of greatness. To deplore it is to deplore the fact that Titian and Rembrandt and Van Gogh painted too much, and that Shakespeare, Balzac, and Goethe had graphomania. Of course there are some weaker Titians, Rembrandts, and Van Goghs, some minor works of Shakespeare, Goethe, and Balzac, just as there are mediocre pieces by Bach, Mozart, Haydn, and Beethoven. Even the most independent of geniuses must pay some tribute to his time. But without the steady exercise of the hand, or the constant outward obligation or inner urge to produce, we should have master works neither by Rembrandt nor by Bach. Wagner found a substitute for the routine of daily 'practice' in the enormous extent of his works; all his works from *Rienzi* to *Lohengrin* are, as it were, rungs of the technical ladder which he had to mount, one by one. The same was true, after accumulated experience in life and suffering, of the operas from *Rheingold* to *Parsifal*. Wagner 'corrected' but little in his earlier works, excepting the 'Faust Overture' and *Tannhäuser;* and in reality only the later version of the 'Faust Overture' can be regarded as having been dictated by his artistic conscience. This is not saying that there was nothing to be corrected in the earlier works. The opinion that Wagner always produced the highest, the unimprovable, which has become orthodox, is due solely to the robust egotism of Wagner, his contempt for the critics, and the uncritical tolerance of his admirers through two generations.

It was Hugo Wolf's lack of craftsmanship, and not only venereal disease, that ruined one of the best Wagnerians and one of the most inspired musicians —that prevented him from converting the dead pauses in his productions into live ones, and caused the 'cramp' in so many of his songs. In the case of Berlioz and Schumann, the fact that they learned the craft so late took its toll from their works; and it was one of the greatest pieces of luck in the life of that perpetual college student, Richard Strauss, that his father was a horn player in the Court Orchestra of Munich. With Strauss, craftsmanship

amounts almost to genius. What Strauss has written during his last decades is—to use Gustav Mahler's phrase concerning Puccini's *Tosca*—'master-
jobbery' (*Meistermachwerk*).

There are, of course, many writers who are too
prolific, and the more they write, the further removed they are from greatness. A beautiful contemporary example is the aging Richard Strauss—
the opposite to Haydn, or Verdi, or Wagner, who
sublimated their genius in their old age, while Richard Strauss descended from the quasi-genius of his
early period to the genius-like handicraft of his later
years. Between the 'graphomania' of the great and
the not-great composers there is one important difference: with the great ones it is mainly due to the
inner urge to produce, to their *demoniacal* industry.
Nothing forced Bach to write—along with the
works commissioned by the Coethen court and the
churches in which he was permanently engaged,
along with his cantatas and Passions, along with his
sonatas and concertos—the *Inventions,* the *Well-
tempered Clavichord* and the *Art of Fugue.* It was
this same demoniacal urge that caused the decisive
step in Handel's artistic career, the step without
which he might have become only the first among

many, but not Handel. I refer to the change from opera composer to creator of oratorios. In those days Handel must have visualized a new, more powerful and extensive following, for which he had to create: no longer the nobility, no longer a caste which accepted his anthems and operas, but a nation and —in the *Messiah*—a Christian community, a pious congregation which comprised more than one denomination. He was no longer young when he conceived this thought and made this decision; he could have had a more comfortable time; but he deliberately assumed this task.

Gluck's case is not dissimilar. To all appearances he belongs to the 'comfortable' composers. There are years, after his rich marriage, in which he takes his ease and produces nothing. But ambition and cupidity do not suffice to explain his setting forth once again, as an old man, to conquer Paris, to brave a thousand obstacles, struggles, excitements.

In Mozart the inner compulsion becomes most evident when, around 1782, he gets to know the works of Bach—the *Well-tempered Clavichord,* the *Art of Fugue,* the Organ Trios. As a child of the eighteenth century, he was purely a composer 'on order'; only in a few works, such as the famous six 'Haydn' quartets, he seems to have created in response to his artistic urge. In reality he always followed the artistic urge; he was so full of 'figure' (to use an expression of Albrecht Dürer) that he was grateful for any excuse or outward impulse. How hungry he was, all through his life, for a *scrittura*—the commission to write an opera! But when, as for instance between 1787 and 1789, none made its appearance, he could, of course, not write an opera. The new acquaintance with Bach, with a gigantic musical power such as his own period did not offer, caused a fearful crisis in his creative career. Here was a style that was greater, more self-contained, more perfect than any of his own time. He might have ignored it as being outmoded; even before 1782 he had written works of ultimate perfection in his own style. But he did not ignore it: he worked, he 'speculated' (his own expression) until he had squared accounts with Bach. That is the demoniacal industry we mean, not the mere fecundity of a Telemann or a Boccherini.

Fundamentally, it is the same industry which forced Beethoven to search, in a hundred variants —the so-called sketches—for the definitive, the valid form for his thoughts. But this demoniacal industry no longer expresses itself quite so unequivocally with him and the musicians of the nineteenth century, because it is difficult to decide with what other ingredients it is mixed—in Beethoven's case a high-spirited determination to excel predecessors and rivals. But it does exist—in every great composer, even in the nineteenth century.

o 2 o

AND so we have reached the question of the difference between genius and talent, which in music as in other things is not a quantitative but a qualitative difference. Just as in the graphic arts there is no gradual merging from Bandinelli to Michelangelo, so that, say, a somewhat better 'Bandinelli' might anyhow be a weaker 'Michelangelo,' so in music there is no bridge between Telemann and Bach, between Bononcini and Handel, between Kozeluch and Haydn, between Paesiello and Mozart, between Cherubini and Beethoven, between Tomaschek and Schubert, between Meyerbeer and Wagner, between Donizetti and Verdi. What we are dealing with is the great secret of *personality,* for the study of which the example of the 'plagiarist' Handel may perhaps be most suitable. No one knew about Handel's plagiarizing of Stradella, Erba, Urio, and others, until a great Handel admirer, Chrysander, discovered it. Since then several naive and well-meaning people have taken the trouble to defend Handel the plagiarist, and to adduce extenuating circumstances in his favor—on the ground that in his period people did not take an authorship-theft so seriously as today. That defense is as correct as it is unnecessary. Handel *made* something out of his thefts, he usurped others' property not only as a mighty conqueror, but he made a usurer's profit out of it; and even where he copied, so to speak, word for word, the copy became, *in* and *through* the new context, his property. Gluck, the other great conqueror of the eighteenth century, has done similar things, with his own as well as others' works. The strongest of all personalities is that of Johann Sebastian Bach, in whose hands arrangements, 'after' Legrenzi or Vivaldi, become appropriations (in the literal sense) and almost original works.

There are people (one might call them myopic) who may agree with our juxtaposition of Handel with Bononcini or Porpora, but who will not accept the greatness-equation Bach-Handel. It is instruc-

tive to confront the despisers and admirers of Handel
with one another: on the one hand Liszt and Wagner and their disciples; on the other hand Mozart,
Beethoven, Brahms. It is true, Handel—especially
Handel, the instrumental composer—must be regarded as the inferior whenever the detailed construction of a work, the chiselling of details is considered. But the juxtaposition of Bach and Handel,
the designation of a 'Bach-Handel period,' is not
really valid at all. They are completely incommensurable. Bach was an organist, an instrumental-
ist of the most personal kind, not merely 'German,'
but a musician *sui generis*. Handel, however, was
a vocal composer, an Italian composer—the greatest
'Italian' of his time—the heir of Alessandro Scarlatti
and Corelli. It is rather childish to make fun (as
has been done) of Handel's vocal themes such as
the end of the *Messiah:* 'Blessing and honor, glory
and pow'r be unto Him,' or similar ones in *Joshua*
and *Judas Maccabæus*. Handel's counterpoint, Handel's polyphony, has quite different roots from
Bach's. And Handel's polyphony and melodic style
do not rank below, but beside Bach's.

° 3 °

WHAT distinguishes genius from talent is condensation, which is related to brevity but is not identical with it. What Bach did to his material was nothing but condensation, a stronger vitalization through musical energy and expression—musical, not poetic expression, it must be noted—through a deeper fullness of musical symbolism. Beethoven presumably meant the same thing when he is alleged to have said that music was 'writing poetry in tones.' Writing poetry (*dichten*) is in reality condensing (*verdichten*), and not composing according to a program —either prescribed or original—by means of which one might make Beethoven easier to grasp and understand (as has been tried, on the basis of Beethoven's own remark).

If Bach had not been born, the leading representative of German music in the first half of the eighteenth century would be Georg Philipp Telemann, of Magdeburg—Bach's senior by four years and his survivor by seventeen, a happy and successful man. He far exceeded Bach in productivity, and like Bach (and later Mozart) he was a man that could write in all manner of styles, in the French as well as the Italian. But when he wrote in these styles there was always a residue of imitation, albeit tasteful imitation. When Bach wrote a concerto *'im italienischen Gusto,'* it was Bachian or, as has been incorrectly said, German. For it was not his so-called Germanism that determined Bach's style; rather it was Bach's music that determined the German style. A national style is the sum of the individualities of speech that can be drawn from the work of musicians—but sometimes can *not* be drawn from it; for if Bach is German, then the Wagner of *Tristan* or *Parsifal* is definitely not very German. Bach just is Bachian, and Wagner Wagnerian.

The process of condensation becomes very clear when we compare Mozart with his Italian contemporaries. 'Mozart and Cimarosa'—that doesn't go, even if Stendhal believed it did. Berlioz was absolutely right when in an annotation to his memoirs of this corpulent consul at Civitavecchia he said that he 'wrote the most irritating lucubrations on music, for which he fancied he had some feeling.' Mozart had the good fortune—and merit—to have captured, in *Nozze di Figaro, Don Giovanni,* and even *Così fan tutte,* some of the best librettos which Italian opera of those days afforded. But not the very best. The very best *opera buffa* librettos, in the Vienna of Mozart's time, were not written by Da Ponte but by Giovanni Battista Casti, his rival, who unfortunately plays about the same role in the history of Italian literature of the eighteenth century as Pietro Aretino did in the sixteenth. He wrote a number of *novelle galanti* which are as salacious as they are witty—but, after all, perhaps more witty than salacious. Byron must have known them and admired them; otherwise we should hardly have his *Don Juan*. Goethe, in any case, was freer from prejudice than the hypocritical nineteenth and twentieth centuries. On 17 July 1787, he was dining with Count Friess in Rome, and reported: 'Abbate Casti, who travels with him, recited one of his novels, the *Archbishop of Prague*, which is not very decent but most beautifully set in *ottave rime*. I already respected him greatly as the author of my beloved *Rè Teodoro in Venezia*. He has now written a *Rè Teodoro in Corsica*, of which I have read the first act—also a most delightfully charming work.' This judgment weighs much more than the unfavorable one of Casanova, who simply hated

Casti from the ground up, because he must have recognized in him the far superior mind.

King Theodore in Corsica seems to have been lost; but in naming *King Theodore in Venice* we name the best libretto of the time—not a perfect work, for perfection in the field of the libretto was neither attempted nor attained. The fate of the German adventurer, Baron Neuhof, who at one time was actually made king by the Corsicans, had already been immortalized in an episode of Voltaire's *Candide,* and Casti used the subject for an *opera buffa* which is tragi-comical, but in quite a different sense from *Don Giovanni.* In *Don Giovanni* buffoonery is one of the ingredients of tragedy—the tragedy of Donna Anna's fate—and there always remains an unresolved residue of this mixture. The dethroned king, a genuine king without money, who ends up in the debtors' dungeon, is a hero of a real tragi-comedy, and the tragic element is doubly poignant and painful under its shell of burlesque. The *Rè Teodoro,* which had its première in Vienna in 1784, first gave Mozart and Da Ponte the courage to attempt the setting of a 'topical' subject like *Nozze di Figaro.* But the enmity between

Da Ponte and Casti robbed the world of one of its
greatest masterworks. For unfortunately it was not
Mozart who set *Rè Teodoro,* but Giovanni Paesiello.
Very nicely composed, very vivacious, without any
faults of style. But just because it is faultless in
style, it is inadequate and therefore not great. The
work had a great success in its time, in Germany, in
Paris, and in London—also in Italy. But any attempt to revive it would end, despite the quality of
the libretto, in a complete fiasco. It lacks what we
have called 'condensation.' Paesiello said everything
in a broader and a more shallow way than Mozart,
and abbreviations and cuts would not do the least
bit of good. A brilliant libretto, a perfect lyric poem
must fall into the hands of the right musician.
Twenty musicians, including Berlioz, composed
Goethe's *Gretchen am Spinnrad.* Of all of them the
only successful and adequate setting is Schubert's.
Hugo Wolf and Brahms both fought shy of composing Goethe's (or rather Marianne Willemer's)
second song of Suleika, *Was bedeutet die Bewe-
gung,* after Schubert had composed it. Richard
Wagner did not hesitate a moment to sell the text
of his *Flying Dutchman* to the Paris Opera. He

knew that Monsieur Pierre Louis-Philippe Dietsch
would not be able to compose it in the only way in
which it had to be composed.

° 4 °

THE comparison of Beethoven with Cherubini leads
to the examination of another example of the problem 'genius versus talent.' Beethoven greatly esteemed Cherubini—alone among his contemporaries
—as a model and as a stimulator, and justly so.
For Cherubini was a master of the highest rank.
Without Cherubini's *Les deux journées* and his
Mass in C minor, neither *Fidelio* nor the *Missa
solemnis* would have been created; without Cherubini's overtures, no *Leonora Overture*. Cherubini is
related to Beethoven in a remarkable way: as a master who stands completely above nationality, as a
musician of whose Italianism nothing remained but
the most subtle feeling for vocal quality; as one who
was equally a disciple of Gluck and of the French
masters of the *opéra comique,* and a disciple of
Haydn, the writer of quartets. Philipp Spitta expressed it perfectly when he recommended the pur-

(134)

chase of Cherubini's posthumous works, in an expert opinion for the Prussian State Library: *

The approach to an understanding of [a composer's] individuality by way of the national character is, as it were, completely barred in the case of this man. Cherubini offers the phenomenon—doubly remarkable in an Italian—of a cosmopolitan musician. Born in Florence and educated in the school of the Bolognese Sarti, strictly and thoroughly trained in the forms of Old Italian church music to the same degree as he was made familiar with the light and deftly constructed opera music of his contemporary compatriots, he nevertheless wrote his most numerous and important works for the artistic institutions of Paris, which had become his second home; and he finally received his most effective influences from the study of the great German masters of his time. This explains the fact that while Italians as well as Frenchmen and Germans find isolated familiar characteristics in his works, on the whole these awaken a feeling of strangeness at first. The various elements which permit us to recognize his musical personality do not, on the surface, appear to be welded together; indeed, nothing lay further from the master than a futile striving for the applause of the cultivated public of every

* Schemann: *Cherubini,* p. 704.

nation, by bringing something to each. It was the innermost compulsion of a serious and thoughtful nature that caused him to marshal everything in the culture of the peoples that might be useful to him for the development of his own individuality. All this he fused into a more than commonly incomparable, significant tonal idiom peculiar to himself alone. But, in consequence, he has sacrificed all that sympathy which, being based on nationality, forcibly brings hearts and minds together [*die Gemüter zueinander zwingt*].

All that is equally true of a compatriot of Cherubini—if one considers a man from Ferrara as the compatriot of one from Florence—namely Girolamo Frescobaldi. It is very significant that there is as yet no Italian Complete Edition of the works of Frescobaldi, and that most notice has been taken of him in Germany. Frescobaldi is one of the greatest Italian musicians, and nothing about him is 'Italian.' He merged northern and southern elements into a perfect personal unity; but there is in his musical personality nothing of melodic softness, colorfulness, or what the Germans call *Schmelz*. Everything in his music is constructive and fanciful in a Nordic— not a *baroque*—sense. The true spiritual pupils and followers of Frescobaldi are Froberger, Buxtehude, Lübeck, and Bach. He is one of the many who bear witness against the assertion of the 'racial experts' that polyphony is a monopoly of the Nordic musical peoples, while luscious melody and homophony are exclusive to the musical nations of the south.

All this is in equal measure true of Beethoven, who also created for himself a tonal idiom at once individual, personal and universal, in which nothing is 'Flemish' or 'Rhenish' or 'Viennese,' nothing 'German,' but everything Beethovenian. For the concept 'German music' has been formed after the work of the great masters, and not the other way about. When Beethoven utilizes Russian themes in the three string quartets, opus 59, they completely lose their character as folk music, and become Beethovenian. In this case the thematic material is material with a particular hall-mark, but it is just material. Changed from the 'Russian' into the Beethovenian, its 'folk' quality no longer attracts one's attention. In a later period the particular point and charm of national melodies, or national turns of phrase, lie precisely in the emphasis on their particular flavor. Cherubini and Beethoven still lived in the happy age when it was possible to coin a universal musical idiom without falling into abstractions, or into emptiness.

But Beethoven was the stronger, the more personal of the two. We remember Cherubini's remark, when, at a concert of the Société des Concerts, one of his overtures was to be performed along with a Beethoven symphony: 'I shall stand there as just a little fellow.' * Beethoven's work is more 'condensed.' There are six string quartets by Cherubini dating from different periods, and one of them, in E-flat major, which is occasionally performed, is so original and at the same time so masterly in its facture that one eagerly reaches for the others—only to put them down again, disappointed. Cherubini has accomplished something particular only in this one case. 'How good that is—for Cherubini!' one exclaims, while, in the case of one of the seventeen quartets of Beethoven, the one marked opus 74, one has a secret and embarrassed desire to confess: 'What a weak Beethoven!' That is the difference. The rule that one should judge a master by his highest accomplishments is not quite right. We must judge him by *all* his accomplishments. It sometimes hap-

* Miel: *Notice sur la vie et les ouvrages de Cherubini*, p. 29.

(138)

pens that a work is 'accomplished,' or even perfect, without its creator being great; it sometimes happens that an amateur turns out a song for which a master might envy him—just as a homely woman may sometimes give birth to a pretty child. In music, however, even such a stroke of good fortune requires technical mastery. The 'surprising' Cherubini quartet was possible only in the case of a musician who had written the *Anacreon* overture and the Requiem in C minor. If the *Unfinished* were the only Schubert work to have come down to us, we should have to conclude that a musician who had created that must have written works like the string quartet in A minor, the quintet in C major or the Suleika song in B minor. In poetry, where the language is the same medium as that in which the amateur thinks and writes, an accidental 'masterpiece' is thinkable, and sometimes a fact; but not in music.

° 5 °

UNIVERSALITY is a part of real greatness. Universality in a twofold sense: either in the sense of command over all, or at least many, regions of music; or in the sense that even as a specialist the musician

creates a new world concept—a permanent enrich-
ment of our inner being which functions and fructi-
fies on and on. Palestrina appears to be a specialist in comparison with Orlando di Lasso, but he
was by no means only an ecclesiastical composer.
Marenzio, the great master and specialist of the
madrigal, also wrote masterly ecclesiastical works.
Monteverdi's universality is so palpable that one
needs only to point to the extreme boundaries of his
life work, the *Sancta Maria* written for St. Mark's
in Venice, and the *Incoronazione di Poppea,* composed for the Teatro SS. Giovanni e Paolo—not to
mention the composer's development, from the
Madrigali spirituali of 1583 to the *Selva morale e
spirituale* of 1641. And think of Bach, who develops
from a single root—that of the organ—a creation
which comprises a hundred different vocal and instrumental forms. Haydn was decidedly an instrumental composer, but he nevertheless wrote a few
memorable masses and oratorios, both sacred and
secular, which make it impossible to reduce him to
a single and unique formula. The most universal of
all masters is Mozart. Where lies the summit of his
art? In the concertos for piano, in the string quartets, or in his comic operas? Was he more of an

instrumental than a vocal composer? Beethoven is
more one-sided, among other things, because vocal
music is less close to him than instrumental; while
with Schubert, again, it is difficult to decide whether
to place the creator of the songs higher than the
composer of the B-minor symphony, the D-minor
string quartet, and the posthumous piano sonata in
B flat, or the other way around.

In the nineteenth century one single species suffices for the creation of a musical cosmos. We should
wonder at Verdi in the guise of symphonist, just as
we still wonder today at his string quartet. Wagner
loses nothing from the fact that we remember his
'pure' orchestral works—the *Faust Overture,* the
Kaisermarsch, and even the *March of Homage,*
which are all minor works, for he always needed the
stimulus of the word and the scene. But his entire
cosmos is enclosed within his dramatic creations,
and it would be so even if he had written nothing
beyond *Tristan and Isolde.* On the other hand, we
have lost nothing by the fact that Brahms could
not write an opera, even though he imagined that
he did not get around to it for purely external reasons. He is sufficiently 'universal' without it. Even a
specialist of the song, Hugo Wolf, has the urge to

universality, and writes a quartet, a symphonic poem, an opera, because without them his cosmos would not be rounded off. There is no greater specialist than Chopin: he could not trust his cosmos to any other vehicle than the piano; but it is a cosmos as extensive as that of another great master, and we could hardly dispense with one of his works—none of the sonatas, none of the dances and nocturnes, none of the études. A contrary example is Domenico Scarlatti, an enchanting composer, full of *esprit*, whimsicality, invention, a composer without whom we can hardly picture for ourselves the frank gaiety, the bizarre charm, the wit of the eighteenth century —a precious possession of music, like a ring with a glistening stone. But he has only a few types of invention; it suffices if we know 30 out of his 550 sonatas, just as it is enough to have seen three pictures by Francesco Albani. The same is true of Corelli, who is a specialist, despite his enormous international influence on an entire century, and who created only a narrow and small, even though a very high-bred and noble world; while his predecessor, Giacomo Carissimi, who never wrote an instrumental work, is likewise one of the great masters. The same is true of Couperin and Rameau. Couperin was well-named 'le Grand'; and Rameau is a first-class master of style, whether he writes piano pieces or orchestral dances or operas. But mastery of style does not suffice for greatness if we do not discover the great human content behind the perfection of style, and if, within the conventional frame—be it ever so delicate and charming—we do not see the countenance. Purcell is great, although a lesser master of style; and Debussy, the admirer of Rameau, is in a certain sense great: neither stylization nor his originality has barred him from near-greatness.

Berlioz, who—it is true—has ridden his colt in all the fields of music and may therefore be called universal, may at the same time be considered one of the most one-sided of musicians, because of the predominance of the descriptive element, the accentuation of color in his work. An unharmonically inclined musician, too, may be very great—if he succeeds in 'compensating' his shortcoming, so long as he forms his cosmos after a vision that is his own. Once again it is Wagner who has managed to do this in the most magnificent way; for Wagner, not being a musician born to the craft, only *used* music for his purposes—as the most powerful means to excitement and effect. Like all romanticists he was, as a musician, primarily a harmonist and colorist; the melodic and rhythmic elements were not so strongly developed in him, and occupy only a secondary place. Compare him with Bach and Mozart, in whom the three components of the musical language are present in perfect balance, no matter how strongly they may accentuate, or how boldly they may employ any one of the three. It has often been pointed out that Mozart was a much more inventive pioneer in the field of harmony than Beethoven, for Beethoven's speech culminates in rhythm. Beethoven, the self-disciplinarian, never exceeds the point in harmony where it might function as a luxury, or become an end in itself.

The harmful kinds of one-sidedness became prominent only at the end of the nineteenth century. There is a German composer by the name of Max Reger with whom harmony and the disease of modulation was heightened to monstrous proportions, while the rhythm was so devitalized as to become amorphous. It would be difficult, indeed, to classify him as 'great,' although it has happened in Germany, still happens, and may happen several times more. Claude Debussy stands just barely at the periphery of greatness because he cultivated his harmonic mannerism too much. Bizet, on the other hand, in a smaller format, is the happiest and most delightful example of the perfect balance of talents: harmony, rhythm, and melody (including some fine flashes of polyphonic imagination) are with him equally developed and fused into a nice unity. (Our present misfortune, 'modernistic' music—a misfortune of which we shall speak in the second part of this book—is especially marked in that the components of music have, as it were, parted company and fled into the distant corners—or, scientifically expressed, have isolated themselves in the manner in which chemical elements are 'isolated.') But water can be produced only through the association of H_2O—oxygen and hydrogen.

o 6 o

THERE was a time when originality was considered one of the conditions for greatness. An early example is German poetry of the second half of the eighteenth century, when the country teemed with 'original geniuses,' namely young poets who with the help of Shakespeare and Rousseau shook off all the traditional rules of art. Goethe began life as such an original genius, with his *Götz von Berlichingen* and *The Sorrows of Werther*. But he did not end up as an original genius. He became a wise master of his art; and his mature works reflect the experience and the influence of universal literature. And the classicism of these works provoked the smiles and petty criticism of the new 'romantics.' It was the same with Shakespeare, who began with *Titus Andronicus* and ended with *The Tempest*.

There is no parallel to Shakespeare and Goethe in music, unless we see one in Robert Schumann, who launched his ship in the youthful stream of originality but sailed towards the broader reaches in the symphonic and choral works of his later years. But if one considers the three souls in his breast— the fiery Florestan, the intimate, inward Eusebius, and the thoughtful Raro—one finds that Florestan was too quickly consumed in a sort of spontaneous combustion, that Raro was deficient both in wisdom and brilliance, while the inwardness of Eusebius often became sheer sentimentality. Every master, of course, goes through a process of clarification, which distinguishes his late from his early work, and which has nothing to do with originality. The 'middle' Verdi—the Verdi of *Aida*—no longer displays the melodic explosive power of *Trovatore;* and the Verdi of *Otello* and *Falstaff* no longer has the sensuous amplitude of *Aida*. His melodic line has become thinner and paler. Nor has the greater or lesser consciousness—a means of distinguishing the 'naive' from the 'intellectual' musicians—anything to do with originality. The original musician is not the more naive. There is no such thing in music as 'naive creation' and it is a moot question whether anything of the kind exists in the other arts. It is most significant that the popular belief in 'musical inspiration,' i.e., a sort of divine revelation, is upheld especially by 'romantic' artists—that atavistic species which claims relationship with the great founders of religions—those 'appointed ones' who received the revelation of truth as a present from a higher power, as Moses received the Thora and Mohammed the Koran. As is well known, the question whether these were indeed revelations has been widely disputed.

The process of creation is a mixture of the conscious and the unconscious, of male and female, of dullness and enlightenment, which is easily comprehended in the artist's own experience, but which practically defies analysis. If one wants to regard

Schubert as one of the most naive of musicians, and see an especially naive, 'celestial' inspiration in the second theme of the first movement of the *Unfinished,* closer examination may reveal that the originality, the naïveté of this *Ländler* theme is not a sudden fancy, but the introduction into a symphonic work, hence, perhaps, a very conscious act. Accordingly, too, the symphonic transformation and application of this theme is a very deliberate process. Here Schubert does what Haydn had done fifty or sixty years before: he introduced a 'heterogeneous' element into instrumental music—a popular note, the Upper Austrian or Lower Austrian—as something material and unstylized. For this innovation North German critics found great fault with Haydn as having done something 'unworthy' of art, and certain critics still find the same fault today. It would be naive to believe that Haydn did not know what he was doing—the same Haydn who wrote on the margin of a contrapuntal passage in one of his manuscripts: 'This is for all-too-learnèd ears.' Haydn's originality lay in his artistic intelligence, and in his courage.

Originality sinks in value if one considers that none of the great masters was original in the sense

that Domenico Scarlatti, John Field, or Edvard
Grieg were original. Bach was not original; he was
a great imitator and appropriator. Otherwise the
dispute concerning the genuineness or spuriousness
of so many of his works would not have arisen.
Mozart was not original; he was a great 'learner,' a
pupil of Johann Christian Bach, of Michael and
Joseph Haydn, of Mysliveczek and other Italian or
Italianate masters. He was, in short, a great amalga-
mator. Beethoven's originality, which is a kind of
high spirits, changed with the course of years into
that supreme unconcern for the world and its appreciation, which the 'empirical' Beethoven regretted
so naively later on.

The fact that originality or, let us say, originality
at first blush has nothing to do with greatness is
most aptly proven by Wagner, who became original
only as his work progressed. Indeed, one may *become* original: and every great master becomes original if he is not content with mere exploitation of his
talent—his particular personal 'note.' Wagner's pat-
rimony as a pure musician was ridiculously small.
If one examines his opus 1, the piano sonata in
B flat, one feels like blushing at its utter lack of
invention and aptitude; and it is a long time—until

(149)

Lohengrin—before the musician Wagner catches up with the dramatist Wagner, by way of Weber and Marschner, Hérold and Meyerbeer, and even Rossini and Bellini. The inner growth of Wagner the musician to something beyond himself, and through his own resources, is one of the most curious and wonderful processes, leading to the attainment of that personal idiom which is so inimitable and alas! so widely imitated. Its impulse is Wagner's demoniacal will to power, which demands the strongest effects in music—music as the most powerful ingredient in that 'accumulated measure of sensual aggression' (one of Thomas Mann's phrases) which Wagner considered necessary for the conquest of his listener. Its vital organ is Wagner's tremendous intellectuality; and both together, the will to power and the intellectuality, constituting the unconscious-conscious, produced that climax and turning point in music whose name is *Tristan*. And the increase in Wagner's originality continues uninterruptedly to the end. *Parsifal* is, in spite—or just because— of the above-mentioned amalgamation of Catholic elements, his most original, most personal work. There is no greater error than to regard *Parsifal* as the work not of Wagner but of a Wagnerian—a dictum of which unfortunately Gustav Mahler is guilty. If there were such a thing it would be more true of certain places in *Götterdämmerung*, which are purely intellectual combinations of motives. In *Parsifal*, a work of the greatest artistic sagacity, there is nothing of this kind: here the most delicate harmonic allusion, the smallest interval, speaks; here, with the minimum of effort, Wagner achieves the maximum of spiritual effect. Nietzsche, who both loved and hated Wagner, has expressed it most perfectly—Nietzsche, who hated particularly the tendency of the *Bühnenweihe-Festspiel*, the 'Stage Dedication Festival Play,' as a negation of all his own feeling and deepest desire. He says: '*Parsifal* will forever maintain its rank in the art of seduction, as *the* stroke of genius in seduction . . . I admire this work, I should like to have created it myself; but, not having created it, I *understand* it . . . Wagner was never more inspired than at the end. Here the combination of sophistication [*raffinement*], beauty, and morbidity reaches a degree which, as it were, overshadows all Wagner's earlier art . . .' A great artist, and especially an artist like Wagner, who did not begin as a pure musician and who was oppressed by such a plethora of gifts, can *acquire* originality. Wagner did just that.

Wagner is the most irrefutable proof that one may not only begin but end by being original. But another proof—it is obvious that we care nothing about chronological order—is Mozart. How could he, the *Wunderkind,* have begun by being original? All that a child prodigy can do is imitate, more or less cleverly or deceptively, the available models. And prodigies who compose always imitate the most modern models, because otherwise they would not be prodigies. Mozart did this very thoroughly— so thoroughly that one may check up his successively latest models from week to week, as has in fact been done by two able Mozart researchers, Théodore de Wyzewa and G. de Saint-Foix. For decades a symphony by Carl Friedrich Abel passed for a genuine Mozart work; an aria or a piano sonata by Johann Christian Bach strikes us even today as so pre-Mozartian that it would be difficult to distinguish it from a genuine product of Mozart's youth. But by the age of about twenty-five, Mozart had learned his lesson. He had absorbed Haydn and Bach; and he was already speaking his own language, a language that was often quite inconvenient for his contemporaries. It is difficult for us today to see how different it was; we like to regard Mozart as a rival of Paesiello or Martin or Salieri. But from the reaction of his contemporaries we realize how original he had become. Original in a different sense from Haydn, who astonished, amused, and charmed the people of his time by the freshness, wit, and insouciance of his ideas. Mozart seems never to want to exceed the bounds of convention. He wanted to *fulfil* the laws, not to violate them. Yet he constantly violates the spirit of the music of the eighteenth century—by his seriousness, his amiability (which no longer was the amiability of the *rococo* period), his artistry of combination. Only in this way can we explain the failure of his three Italian *opere buffe*. *Entführung* alone, and perhaps *The Magic Flute*, was successful. That, too, is the real reason why the Mozart concerto, except for the 'pathetic' and military types exemplified in the C minor and the C major (Koechel No. 467), did not become a model for Mozart's successors. A few of the strange opinions on his music expressed by contemporaries are familiar to us, such as the one of Emperor Joseph II, who was an average music-lover for his time. There is the judgment of the Württemberg court musician, Johann Baptist Schaul, preserved in his *Letters on the Taste in Music,* 1809, who says of Mozart's works that they contain good things as well as mediocre, bad, and very bad, for which reason they are not worth all the fuss that his admirers make about them. Schaul thought Mozart's fertility resembled 'an inundation which destroys everything, and jumbles soil and plants, stone, wood, and water all over one another.' The famous 'Haydn quartets' of Mozart were returned to their publisher, Artaria, from Italy with the remark that the edition contained too many printer's errors—which simply referred to some voice-leadings that sounded unaccustomed to Italian ears. Success, it is true, followed eventually, and Mozart's *acquired* originality came to appear as a norm, and as the characteristic idiom of his time.

° 7 °

ONE hall-mark of greatness is the perfection of a master's life work, the rounding-off of his 'œuvre,' which in some mysterious way is related to the creator's predestined age. Mysterious, indeed. I know full well that this idea impinges on the mystical, and I am not inviting anyone to follow my argument further. And yet a general feeling has developed, too, for this idea; otherwise the concept of early fruition, in connection with the early death of a genius, would not have taken root. There is a word for it in German—*Frühvollendung*—which combines the meanings of 'early perfection' and 'early completion'—the perfect cycle of a creative life, like the fruition of an early-flowering and early-maturing plant. It is true that we are in danger of imagining a prematurely interrupted life work to be perfect, completely rounded; that once again we are 'giving meaning to the meaningless,' because our imperfect vision simply does not permit us to grasp history in any other way. In that case it would be a coincidence that Haydn lived just long enough to write his London symphonies and *The Creation*, that Wagner lived just long enough to write *Parsifal*, and Verdi long enough to complete *Falstaff*. And, by the same token, it would simply be due to the blind cruelty and the dumb indifference of nature that Purcell and Mozart had to die at the age of thirty-six, Chopin at thirty-nine, and Schubert at thirty-one. But this cruelty and indifference of nature seem not to function in the realm of the intellect, even in the case of those creators who, though of lesser stature than the great ones, nevertheless reach into the *sphere* of greatness. Pergolesi, dead at twenty-six, accomplished exactly his predestined stint, namely to preserve the eighteenth century from petrification in the 'pre-classical' style, and to open a new avenue to music, that of the 'buffonesque' melodic line. The Michelangelo songs of Hugo Wolf, who was mentally dead at the age of thirty-seven, are a conclusive self-confirmation and an ultimate farewell—completion in the artistic as well as the physical sense. It is as though a creative artist had clairvoyant knowledge of the running-down of the spiritual clockwork within him; he regulates it himself, although it was created by a Higher Clockmaker. A great man who dies young has a premonition of the life-span before him. Mozart and Schubert are the two clearest examples of an overflowing productivity, of a frenzied acceleration in the tempo of creation. Both seemed to know that they could not afford to take their time. Haydn did not write his first quartets until he was twenty-seven—and how far removed these quartets or *divertimenti* still were from what we of today conceive to be a Haydn quartet! Mozart, at the age of twenty-seven had already written the *Elopement from the Serail.* Beethoven, who needed a long preparation despite his extraordinary natural gift, composed his first concerto for piano and orchestra at twenty-five—an age at which Schubert had completed the cycle of songs called *The Beautiful Miller's Daughter.* (We do not, of course, compare Schubert with Beethoven in the symphonic field, in which Schubert, thanks to Beethoven, had an easier row to hoe, but in the field of the song, in which he himself was a pioneer.) *The Magic Flute* appears to us as the work of a ripe old age, as also do Schubert's *Winter's Journey* and the songs assembled under the dreadful title of *Swan Song*—a dreadful title, and yet indicative of the mystical foreknowledge of which we spoke. The Austrian poet, Franz Grillparzer, who pronounced Schubert's funeral oration and wrote the epitaph on Schubert's grave, did not think that with Schubert's death a manifestation of art had found its conclusion, had completed its cycle. 'Here music buried a rich treasure and an even greater hope.' In an empirical sense this was true. But only in an empirical sense. Perhaps Schubert challenged fate in that, shortly before his last illness, he uttered the intention of studying counterpoint assiduously with Simon Sechter—a similar intention to that which Anton Bruckner, much later, actually put into practice. The string quartet in C major, the *Unfinished,* the C-major symphony, the string quartets in A minor and D minor would hardly have been enhanced by a greater experience in 'counterpoint,' and perhaps they might have lost something.

Robert Schumann, differing with Grillparzer, was not of the opinion that Schubert had not completed his life work. In discussing his last works he said that it would be futile to ponder on what Schubert might yet have accomplished. 'He has done enough,' he said, 'and, praise be! how he has striven and *perfected!*' Still more noteworthy and decided was the opinion on predestination in the life of an eminent man expressed by Goethe—Goethe, who reached the age of eighty-three so as to complete that great fragment of poetic creation, *Faust.* In an article—one of his greatest masterpieces in prose— on J. Joachim Winckelmann, who 'discovered' the art of antiquity for Germany, he seems to have regarded Winckelmann's return from Rome as a challenge to fate. 'Already devoted, body and soul, to the life of Italy, he thought every other unbearable; and while his earlier journey into Italy through the most mountainous and rocky part of Tyrol interested and even delighted him, he felt, on the journey back to his fatherland, as though he were being dragged through the Cimmerian Gate, full of fear, and frightened by the impossibility of continuing his way.' Winckelmann was murdered in Trieste by a boy with whom he had been brought into contact through a dark, erotic desire. What does Goethe say about this violent and seemingly meaningless end?

Thus he was taken from this world while poised on the loftiest heights of happiness which he could have wished. . . . We may well call him happy for having risen from the highest summit of human existence to the region of the blessèd, for having been taken from the living by a momentary fright and a fleeting pain. The afflictions of age, the waning of the powers of mind, he did not experience . . . Winckelmann's early passing away has also benefitted us. We are strengthened by the power of his spirit, wafted to us from beyond, which arouses in us the most ardent desire always to continue what he has begun with such love and zeal.

And even more remarkable is the way in which Goethe expressed himself on the early deaths of

Raphael and Kepler. In speaking, on 25 January
1813, about the passing of the poet Wieland, in
whose old age (he died at eighty) 'his beautiful
spiritual gifts had not diminished but enlarged,' he
said: 'Once again, do think carefully about this
circumstance: Raphael was hardly in his thirties,
Kepler in his early forties, *when both made a sudden end of their lives* . . .' The early death of
Raphael, then, is to Goethe equivalent to suicide;
the act of death is, as it were, dictated by a higher
power when the mission of the great one has been
fulfilled. Just as the drone must die when it has
fructified the queen bee. It is clear that Goethe,
too, is unaffected by ordinary human pity, that he
blames no biographical coincidence. The reference
to Kepler seems especially cruel, when one remembers the destitution in which he died. Greatness is
subject to a special law, to a special biographical
logic of events.

This is not contradicted by the fact that greatness
is almost always in particular danger—from illness,
from emotional or mental disturbances. Bach and
Haydn may have enjoyed vigorous health till old
age, though the one became blind and the other
became a dotard as the result of overwork. However,

we are not any too well informed about this—especially about the case of Bach. But we do know about the nervous breakdown of Handel, which he conquered by means of a violent cure; and we know the many tales of Beethoven's ill health. Mozart several times—already in childhood—approached the Gates of Darkness with which he was to become so familiar, as a Freemason, in his later years. Schubert experienced his crisis five years before his death —a crisis without which the *Winterreise* would not have been created. And Wagner's crises, which were due to his nervous condition and which each time shook the very core of his being, occurred at almost regular intervals through his life. Within the span of life which fate concedes them, great men experience things that are only just bearable; and these include the pathological experiences which we are in the habit of grouping under the broad classification 'love' and which are, as we know, especially productive of artistic results—with some masters, for instance Wagner, far into old age. Old age in itself, however, does not with great musicians signify a decrease in creative power. It has sometimes been asserted that one must have planted, before the age of thirty, all the artistic germs which

are capable of development later on; that after this
age limit no new 'ideas' (or inspirations) are possible. This may be true. But the arts which are
affiliated with handicraft, such as painting and
music, often demand a long development of the
germs before the aptitude of the hand is equal to
the will. Originality and mastery are almost incompatible: their co-appearance is the rarest of all rari-
ties. A debut with finished works like Goethe's
Götz von Berlichingen or Byron's *Childe Harold*
has hardly a counterpart in music—not even in
Schumann, although he reaches a summit in that
victorious upward sweep from opus 1 to opus 9,
which is the *Carnaval.* And not even in Chopin.
Every master who lives a long life is subject to transformation, to the recurrent miracle of shedding his
skin. Which of Titian's works stand higher—the
so-called *Sacred and Profane Love* in the Villa
Borghese or the *Crowning with Thorns* in the Munich Pinakothek? Which of Rembrandt's works,
the *Anatomical Theatre of Dr. Tulp* of 1632, or one
of the last self-portraits? People may argue long and
loudly about where the apex of Verdi's creation may
be found—in the explosive operas of the period of
Rigoletto (which in some way Verdi has never sur-

passed); in *Aida* and the Requiem; or in *Falstaff*—
but they will never reach agreement. The proportion of invention and mastery is a different one in
all three periods, but behind them all stands Verdi,
whether the young Verdi, the middle-aged, or the
old. Wagner has never surpassed *Tristan* as his
'completely valid musical conception'; and yet *Tristan* is, as a work of art, only the promise of that
which Wagner fulfils in *Parsifal*. Beethoven never
surpassed the *Eroica*, and the quartet opus 59,
No. 1; yet the last quartets are his most valuable
and most hallowed legacy to humanity.

<h2 style="text-align:center">o 8 o</h2>

GREATNESS means the construction of an inner
world, and the communication of this inner world
to the physical world of humanity. The two belong
together; neither is thinkable without the other.
The strongest feeling and the most vivid imagination are worthless to humanity if they do not mani-
fest themselves; the greatest constructive talent is
worthless if it does not serve a creative power that
is capable of forming a cosmos.

No cosmos is thinkable without strains and

stresses, i.e. antagonistic forces; even an inner world
does not come into being without struggle, without
function and resistance. There is happy and unhappy greatness, just as there are happy and unhappy epochs in art (a subject which we shall deal
with in the historical part of this book). I do not
mean the outward destinies which govern the lives
of artists, which may run a more or less agreeable,
or a more or less tragic, course. Every great artist is,
in a certain sense, happy. He knows the happiness
of creating and successful doing, to which no other
happiness on earth can be compared. And how often
must Schubert, the very poorest in this world's
goods, have tasted this happiness! Yet every great
artist is unhappy, too. He feels an inner resistance
to 'the world,' its incapacity and slowness to *comprehend*. It is true that Goethe, who lived to be
eighty-three and who never in his life lacked bourgeois comforts, did remark in the middle of his life
(1788, in Rome) that 'so far as his person was concerned, he had much happiness, indeed it poured
in to him from all sides'; but at the end of his life
he confessed that he could count the hours of real
happiness in his life on the fingers of one hand.

But this kind of unhappiness has nothing to do

with that great 'antagonist,' that evil spirit or *diabolus* which is found in the cosmos of so many of our great masters, the spirit who, like Mephistopheles, 'wills the evil and always creates the good.' We know but little about the different impulses which produce a great work; but we may perhaps distinguish between a product issuing from the fullness of the urge, and one which derives from the necessity to readjust or repair, by means of art, an inner world that has become disjointed or out of gear. In the graphic arts the example and counterexample are Raphael and Michelangelo; and if the example of Raphael may be badly chosen, Michelangelo at any rate was a *dyskolos,* whose mighty work was conceived in the somberest of moods: even when he exaggerates, when he is 'baroque,' his exaggeration and his baroque are never the result of joy.

And how is it with the great musicians? It seems clear that the 'happy ones' will be found more often in the earlier centuries, and the *dyskoloi* more often in the nineteenth and twentieth; but it only seems so, and caution is advisable. How about Handel? It would be simple to claim for Handel merely his power, his monumentalism, his serenity, or, as his detractors would say, his shallowness and superficiality. But Handel was one of the most secretive of men—one who gave nobody admittance to his inner life—neither by personal contact nor in letters. If we compare what his London contemporaries reported about him with that which they *might* have reported and what they did report about a hundred lesser men, there is nothing left but the most external: some anecdotes about his uncouth manners, his violence, and his gluttony, and then a bit of melodrama about the blindness of his last years. And this concerns a man who stood in the center of public life—in a time and place notorious for publicity without sense of shame! Is there not something mysterious about a man of such extraordinary vitality in whose life, nevertheless, the female sex seems to play no role whatever? Did Handel become one of the greatest Italian composers of his time because he *needed* the purest, most clarified, and rarefied forms, the most typical, impersonal expression of elementary power and traditional beauty?

Indeed, we wholly misunderstand art in general and music in particular if we always interpret it as the 'expression of the spirit of the time.' It *is* that—sometimes, but not always. For instance, was music

an 'expression of the spirit of the time' in the sixteenth century—the century of a religious schism
which cost almost as much blood and misery as
nationalism and racial mania are costing in the
twentieth—the century of the sack of Rome, of St.
Bartholomew's Night, and a never-ending sequence
of wars and epidemics? In reality music is a *coun-
ter*-expression of the spirit of the time. In the sixteenth century, music is not emotional but sedative:
a gift from heaven which lifts up the soul, purifies,
comforts, and pacifies the hearts of men. Is not the
music of the nineteenth century, too, a counter-
expression of the spirit of the time? Certainly this
is true of the music of Richard Wagner—an art
which excites and enraptures the common citizen,
showing him highly modern psychological conflicts
in heroic settings: Are the *Ring of the Nibelung,
Tristan and Isolde, Parsifal* affirmations of the nineteenth century? Are they not rather characteristi-
cally inopportune negations of its trends? Or, to be
more exact, are not these contradictory, heroically
intimate, bi-polar music-dramas, like the whole of
romanticism? Romanticism is the re-construction of
reality, and at the same time a flight from reality.
Wagner's *Parsifal* is the perfect example of this bi-

polarity. It is the flight from sensuality, expressed in music whose deepest roots are hidden in eroticism. Preaching the ideal of asceticism in an opera house! The teachings of St. Francis exhibited before the belated, tired, industrialized, newspaper-reading citizens of the nineteenth century! Art as the substitute for religion! Nothing like this existed before the nineteenth century: such soul-searching, such emotional conflict, the earlier centuries never knew. But they already knew art as a medicine of life, as the image of a purer and higher world of feeling. And so, too, the work of many an earlier epoch, many an earlier master, is due to the inner desire to produce a *corrective,* a counter-image to worldly life.

The musician, the greatest and most incomprehensible of all, who seems to stand outside and above his time and therefore does not need to adjust anything within himself, is Johann Sebastian Bach. When he expresses himself in music, he seems to be not himself, the concert-master of the Coethen court or the choirmaster of a Leipzig church, but music itself. He was an artisan; and it has been said that each week he wrote and performed his church cantata just as a carpenter makes a chair or a goldsmith fashions a goblet. The wonder is that he did not do it more badly: had he done it less well, he would perhaps have fared better with his contemporaries. But his demon forced him to do it as well as possible, regardless of whether anyone recognized and appreciated it or not. Bach, the man, disappears completely behind his work—much more than Shakespeare disappears behind his drama. There is no dispute, no dualism in this music.

In Mozart there is both. This has not always been recognized, least of all in the time between 1814 and 1880, the time of Mendelssohn, Schumann, Wagner, the time of the Jahn biography, which saw in Mozart the incarnation of pure harmony, 'music's genius of light and love.' How very characteristic is the phrase on the first page of the Introduction to Jahn's book, which speaks of Mozart as 'the master who does not bare the working of his passion in the art-work itself, but who evokes beauty in full perfection and purity after all that was impure and troubled has been completely overcome.' That is the point of view of the nineteenth century, the retrospective view from the vantage point of Wagner's time; but it certainly was not the view of the eighteenth century, when Mozart was a revolutionary who aroused the dislike of his Italian contemporaries. All the same, even Jahn admits that the 'pure and perfect beauty' of Mozart's works was the result of purification after a process of fermentation, that the 'impure' and the 'turgid' (*'trübe'*) had to be overcome, before it could assume its perfect form. Impure and turgid? *Can* these attributes be applied to Mozart's soul, as they can be applied to some modern 'romantic' composers, who have to escape into ecstasy because their internal self is unclean and evil—to say it candidly and straight from the shoulder? Mozart's music is always honest; but something personal vibrates in it, which has been called sorrowful or demoniacal. And it has none of the shallowness of the music of Paesiello, Boccherini, or Cimarosa. Beneath the brightly shimmering surface, the stream is very deep. Schubert, too, had something similar in mind when he asked: 'Is there really merry music? I know none.'

The same Schubert, who created that depth of sweetest melancholy which is called *Unfinished Symphony,* said something remarkable about death, when in a letter from Steyr to his father and stepmother (25 July 1825) he remembered his brother Ferdinand: '. . . He will certainly have been ill again 77 times, and 9 times he will have feared he had to die, as though dying were the worst that could happen to human beings. If he could only once see these divine hills and lakes, the sight of which threatens to smother or devour us! He would no longer love this insignificant human life so much; and would consider it a great happiness to be returned once again to the mysterious force that resides in our Mother Earth, to live again.' The good parents must have opened their eyes wide when they read that. While Schubert had to live through his severe syphilitic illness, he wrote the *Müller-Lieder;* when he wrote the *Winterreise* he was, as his friend Spaun relates, 'for some time in a mournful mood and apparently ailing. To my question what was happening within him he only replied: well, you will soon hear and understand. One day he said to me: come to Schober today, I shall sing you a wreath of gruesome songs . . . They have moved me more than any of my previous songs have ever done . . .'

A man cannot be great without touching the periphery of humanity. When Goethe refused Schubert's songs set to his poems, it was presumably not only for the reason that the amplitude of the music appeared to interfere with the poetic word, but be-

cause he felt the 'demon' in them, for he himself
had much too much of this demoniacal, this abys-
mal, element to have it stir him in music. It is to
be supposed that for him there was also too much
of this in Beethoven—but then he knew Beethoven's music only very inadequately. Of the once
fashionable theory concerning the relationship of
genius and insanity this much is true: that all great
men, and also great musicians, touch problems
which their talent does not contemplate; that they
wander near the chasm's edge, so that even their
gaiety has a dark background; that for this unsteadi-
ness of feeling and thinking they must often enough
pay dearly in everyday life. The 'gruesomeness' of
Schubert's *Winterreise* belongs to quite another category than that which had been customary in the
song, the ballad, and the opera before his time. In
his youth, Schubert loved and imitated Johann
Rudolf Zumsteeg, a sensitive musician well known
to Schiller and Goethe. Zumsteeg's most famous
work was the composition of a gruesome ballad in
the pseudo-popular style by G. A. Bürger, *Lenore*—
about a maiden who has blasphemed against Provi-
dence and whose dead lover abducts her, not for the
nuptial bed but for a ride to hell. It is a picturesque

gruesomeness, a German variant of French romanticism as it appears in Berlioz's *Damnation of Faust*. With great creators the dark side of the emotions expresses itself differently; it is spontaneous, and may reveal itself in works and in passages where one least expects it.

This dark side has to do with the peculiar irritability of great musicians. Wilhelm Ostwald has emphasized the fact that even a very small discovery in the field of the natural sciences depends upon concentrated mental exertion. 'However favorable the mental organization of a discoverer,' he says, 'his efforts, in the nature of things, approach the extreme boundaries of human capacity.' How much more this is true of a great musician who, if he is no mere imitator and disciple, has to create a world out of nothingness! Even if, in studying the types of great musicians, we adhere to the traditional four temperaments, we shall find among them—certainly not the phlegmatic, but the choleric, the sanguine, and the melancholy types. Now, surely, there exists no pure specimen of any of these primitive and arbitrarily established types, just as there is no purely masculine man or purely feminine woman, or a wholly good or wholly bad person. But we may be justified in labelling Gluck as choleric, Bach and Wagner as sanguine, and Chopin as melancholy; even though we realize at once that none of these rough types suffices to characterize a really great personality. For the great personality would not be great if he did not comprise more than one type, if he could not change from phases of depression to phases of exaltation; if he did not, in the course of a lifetime, undergo several transformations.

However, there is one thing all great musicians had in common. They were irritable in the highest degree, and with Bach it seems to have been his exaggerated, savage irritability alone that lifted him above philistinism as a man. If Schubert appears to have been less irritable, this was only because his helpless condition forbade it, and this was due to his youth and his poverty. The irritability of Mendelssohn, who truly was a darling of the gods, has been vouched for by all his contemporaries; not to mention the well-known cases of Beethoven, Berlioz, Wagner, and Brahms. I once met in Vienna one of the men who actually used to sit with Brahms in the 'Red Hedgehog.' Lost in a reverie about the old times, he said, with deep conviction: 'That was a *bad* man.' But all this does not mean that a thin skin alone proves a man to be a great musician, or a great conductor. The irritability of the great is caused by the task to which they are committed, and the urge to accomplish that task to the utmost degree.

Beethoven is an example of the hero who conquers that dark and fatal something in an artist's life. Beethoven was a happy master, despite his deafness, his dropsy, and the handicap of a good-for-nothing nephew. There is nothing more mendacious than the popular idea of the tragic 'Titan of the Lower Rhine,' who 'thrust his fist into the jaws of fate' with his Fifth Symphony. Mozart was far more pessimistic, resigned, joyless. Among Beethoven's works, those animated by pure high spirits, pure strength, and pure serenity outweigh all others: there is not one gloomy passage in the Fourth or the Eighth Symphony, the piano trio in E flat, the string quartet opus 59, No. 3—to name only a few masterpieces. But Beethoven, afflicted by traits inherited from his drunkard father and himself in danger of succumbing to drunkenness, needs to exercise power in order to 'prove' himself—needs conflict in order to substantiate his victory. Sometimes he is as profound and somber as Mozart, as for instance in the first movement of the so-called *Kreutzer Sonata;* but while Mozart's somberness is the deep stillness of a hidden mountain lake, Beethoven loves to stir the waters to their depths in order to show the conflict within him. Nothing is more characteristic than the rough violence with which he often interrupts the musical train of thought—a violence which sometimes becomes sheer brutality—a naked *gesture.* The Coda must be the strongest possible affirmation of the leading key, hence its beginning cannot be shifted radically enough to suit him. Such a gesture, for instance, occurs twice in the Coda of the slow movement of the C-minor violin sonata (op. 30, No. 2)—a stone rudely thrown into the A-flat major paradise of this movement. Another gesture of this sort is the outbreak of fury at the end of the scherzo of the piano sonata opus 106; and it is a very dangerous one, since the introduction of this B so near the end of a B-flat movement prevents its being resolved into complete consonance: indeed, Beethoven requires two additional long and long-breathed movements. How tame a musician, how addicted to smooth and gentle transitions is the 'dramatic' Wagner, in comparison with Beethoven in this mood!

° 9 °

THE dualism of the nineteenth century, the period of the romantic and neo-romantic—or whatever one wishes to call these different phases of musical development—lies elsewhere than in the structure of the musician's soul. It lies in the position of music in relation to life itself. Music was no longer a natural expression of life; and the great musicians themselves had been the unwitting cause. Gluck, the 'reformer,' became one of the first offenders when he made what one might call 'ethical' demands on his public—demands beyond the pure enjoyment people took in opera. Nothing of the sort had occurred, as yet, to Handel, to whom the writing of operas culminated in the service to *primi uomini* and *prime donne;* and these prima donnas and *castrati* in their turn stood in the service of the public. Mozart, too, was already too great for his time—but so *secretly* great that his time hardly noticed it. The real man of destiny was Beethoven, who wrote a part of his work for himself alone, or

for an imaginary public. He was so great, so powerful, so compelling, that he was able to *create* a
real public for his work—not, of course, without opposition, as is shown by the story of the first performances of the Ninth Symphony and the last
quartets, and by the reception they received. But
the *Missa Solemnis* is an example of the failures he
had to endure. It is the creation of a believing heart
—even a devout Catholic heart, but it is without a
home, either in church or in the concert-hall. During Mozart's and Haydn's time everything was still
in order in the realm of church music: their serene
and unlengthy masses, litanies, offertories are 'practical' music—music which corresponds exactly to
the bright and unsolemn baroque and rococo
churches of Catholic South Germany, and especially
of Upper and Nether Austria and Upper Bavaria.
As for Protestantism, it has had no living music at
all since the time of Bach; and music has no longer
a true home in the Protestant church. The activity
of the Catholic 'Caecilians,' too, with their fight
against 'rococo' church music and their return to
Palestrina and the sixteenth century, only proves
that the union between the church and creative music has been dissolved.

ESOTERIC GREATNESS

Until the end of the eighteenth century the musician, like the architect, the sculptor, and the painter, stood in the service of Society. He composed for Society, filled the orders of Society, and wrote almost only for 'occasions'—for day-to-day occasions and for special ones. In the sixteenth century not a madrigal was written but for a practical purpose; in the seventeenth, no opera without a *scrittura,* that is, a written contract. Since Beethoven, however, musicians write operas and symphonies which are never performed—into the blue, as it were; for a vacuum. They have 'established' themselves as artists; they have created a disagreement between themselves and 'the world.' They naturally feel that there is a tragic conflict, and they try to reconcile it—to bridge the chasm. Schumann tried it by changing over from his 'egotistical,' subjective piano works to the *Lied,* the choral song, and the oratorio. Wagner, a century ahead of his time, while intensifying his personal style into something still more personal, did not rest until he had 'secured a hearing' for each of his works, or—more truthfully—served it up to an obstreperous public, and maybe forced it down its throat, much as Berlioz did in Paris. But Wagner was more forceful and more successful than Berlioz, who never heard his 'Trojans' completely, and who risked and lost enormous sums in order to have his extravagant scores performed. Since Beethoven, nearly all great musicians have waged a war against their time, and only few of them are supported by their period—or their nation. But this belongs in another context—in the historical part of this book.

o IO o

JUST as an Attic tragedy could not end without a satyr-play, so this chapter cannot end without a section which one might call 'Musicians among Themselves,' since it deals with the one-sidedness of great men—their lack of understanding for the greatness of others. This is by no means confined to musicians; it is likewise found in poets and painters and architects and—philosophers. The most striking example of the last-named category is, perhaps, the savage hatred and the savage obtuseness of Schopenhauer in regard to Hegel. This really is incomprehensible, for while Schopenhauer was quite capable of recognizing Hegel's merits, he seemed to be incapable of doing his rival justice. Such one-sidedness may not be an indispensable condition of greatness, but it is so general that one might call it an unavoidable by-product. One would think that there is not a musician, great or small, whom the figure of Bach does not inspire with a certain awe. Yet Berlioz never missed an opportunity to show his scorn and contempt for this 'pre-historic' master of what he—Berlioz—considered an arid and out-moded art-form, the fugue. In Tchaikovsky's *Memoirs of a Musician* we find a sentence whose profundity can be measured only by the—well, let us say the theme from the Andante cantabile of his Fifth Symphony, or his popular piano concerto. (There is always a qualitative relationship between the literary and the musical utterances of a composer.) Tchaikovsky speaks of Schumann's championship of the young Brahms, and makes the statement that 'great artists rarely possess the gift of unfailing critical instinct; rather do they distinguish themselves by the greatest and often incomprehensible *leniency* towards their colleagues in art.' And he immediately furnishes a beautiful example of this 'leniency' himself. For he writes about Brahms, his contemporary and colleague, thus: 'Time has shown that . . . Brahms did not justify the hopes which

Schumann and musical Germany confided in him. Brahms has remained one of those composers of whom the German school has produced dozens and dozens. He writes fluently, with skill, in pure style, but without a trace of independent originality; he only loses himself in endless variations of classical themes.'

No, great musicians are neither lenient nor uncritical; or, better—neither lenient nor without the sharpest eye for the weaker attributes of their fellows. Tchaikovsky's judgment is not an isolated case; it is typical. One may reverse his sentence, as one does with many proverbs to make them really correct, truthful, and meaningful (though sometimes cruel), and say: great artists distinguish themselves by the greatest and often incomprehensible *lack* of indulgence for their artistic colleagues, and by a truly matchless critical one-sidedness and lack of understanding. This does not mean that great musicians are particularly malicious or narrow-minded people. On the contrary: without intelligence and a little kind-heartedness one cannot be quite great. Even Wagner had this kind-heartedness when it came to animals—dogs and parrots.

But before we try to solve the riddle, it may be instructive to examine a few examples.

One might, indeed, begin with Bach and Handel: Bach, who esteemed Handel most highly, and proposed a personal meeting; and Handel, who does not even consider the proposal worthy of a reply. Bach is the greater, also, in this—that he could appreciate Handel's greatness to the full, however foreign it might be to him. But what motivated Handel's attitude? Lack of understanding, or too deep a recognition? If one accepts Johann Adolf Scheibe, Bach's contemporary and critic, as a composer, one may consider his characterization of Bach as 'worthy' of a great musician. According to him, Bach's music is confused and turgid, 'like the words of a horrid poetaster,' and 'as labored as it is useless, because it fights against common sense.' But perhaps Scheibe was after all more of a critic than a creative musician, for he retracted this publicly expressed opinion of Bach just as publicly; and his retraction is a rare document of repentence, self-conquest, and moral reparation—as rare as it is gracious in form. It is not without reason that Lessing had a good opinion of this man Scheibe.

May we once again recall that well-known pronouncement of Handel about Gluck—re-enforced by a robust oath? Gluck, he said, understood as much about counterpoint as his (Handel's) cook, named Waltz! Handel was completely right. But could Gluck have achieved what he did achieve—the transformation of the opera—if he had known more about counterpoint? Is it not true that a genius makes his greatest virtues of his deficiencies? How much did Handel's counterpoint and his gorgeous melodic invention do for *his* operas? Let us also cite Haydn, who said some of the most beautiful and most stirring words of appreciation about Mozart, but who curtly described Sammartini (his alleged prototype) as a 'scribbler.' Yet Sammartini was by no means a scribbler. And what about his remark concerning the 'Grand Mogul' Beethoven, of whose *Leonora* overture he (Haydn) 'didn't understand a note'? . . . We may as well remain silent about Mozart, in whose family circle tongues were certainly sharp and criticism copious, while Mozart's own letters teem with pitiless and unjust opinions about contemporary colleagues. Even about Haydn he seems to have made unfriendly remarks at the end.

We have already quoted Schubert's opinion of

Weber in an earlier chapter. It was a case similar to that of Handel and Gluck. If Schubert could have understood Weber, he would never have written his futile *Students of Salamanca*, or any of his other operatic attempts, but—neither would he ever have written the *Unfinished*, the D-minor quartet and the *Winterreise*. Louis Spohr has cited the opinion of Zingarelli, director of the Naples Conservatory, concerning Mozart: 'He was not without talents, only he lived too short a time to develop them properly.' Spohr drew the head of a donkey on the margin of this dictum. But Spohr himself could not, throughout his life, get clear with Beethoven's last quartets, and he ticked off the harmonic 'errors' in Rossini's score. What do harmonic errors signify in masterpieces like *Cenerentola* or *L'Italiana in Algeri?* Is it a wonder when Mendelssohn, who according to his own report wrote perfect counterpoint even as a small boy, had the lowest opinion of Berlioz, and Berlioz the lowest opinion of Bach and Handel?

As is to be expected, the Wagner circle and Wagner himself built the highest and thickest walls. Heinrich Dorn, court opera conductor in Berlin and himself the composer of a 'Nibelung' opera, wrote

after the first Berlin performance of *Tristan:*
'. . . The most unfortunate text which has ever
been set to music by an important composer . . .'
The famous English-horn solo at the opening of the
third act he called an 'insane fantasy on the *Schalmei*
—a virtuoso piece for an English-horn player confined in the *maison de santé* . . .' Dorn was not a
great musician, but anyhow a musician, and a friend
of Wagner's youth . . . What malicious things
Wagner himself wrote about most of his contemporaries, especially about Brahms, is well known. But
what Brahms said about Wagner is wrong-headed,
too. Brahms considered himself the 'best Wagnerian,' and claimed for himself the ability to understand Wagner better than any of the *musicians* of
his time. But that precisely does not make one a
'Wagnerian.' Wagner was not just a musician and
therefore cannot be understood as a musician alone.

Does anyone remember Brahms' remark about the
'lack of education and insanity' of Bruckner? In
1895 Brahms held forth about Bruckner to a friend
(Dr. Heinrich Groeber): 'Everything with him is
manufactured—everything is affected, nothing natural. His piety—that is his affair; that does not

concern me. But these Mass vacillations [*Mess-Vel-leitäten*] disgust me; I loathe them. He had not a shimmer of musical logic [*Folgerichtigkeit*], no idea of orderly musical construction.' About the same time he said (to Richard Specht): 'In the case of Bruckner we have to do with a fraud, who will be dead and forgotten in one or two years . . . Do you really think that a man could understand even the least of these symphonic snake-monsters among all this unripe mass? . . . Bruckner's works immortal?—or perhaps even symphonies? It is to laugh!'

Bruckner himself was defenseless; he was too timid and too 'uneducated.' But, by way of compensation, here are the words of a Brucknerian, Hugo Wolf, describing Brahms' last symphony: 'True, Brahms' production has never been able to soar above the level of mediocrity; but the nothingness, hollowness, and hypocrisy [*Duckmäuserei*] which dominate the E-minor symphony have never before appeared so ominously in his works.'

Now, if we add a quotation from Tchaikovsky's estimate of *Aida*, the procession of the great has—at least externally—come to an end. He says:

When recently I looked—with understandable prejudice—into the gorgeously printed piano score of *Aida,* I was agreeably surprised to find, in the very first bars of the Introduction, which has been written under strong Wagnerian influence, an unusual charm of harmonic combination, as well as a melodic originality which [however] borders on affectation. I then examined the whole score with the greatest care; and sadly I pondered on the damaging influence that has been exerted on the maestro by the esthetically so unexacting Italian public, for whom Verdi primarily writes his operas. What could not have become of Verdi if in his early years, when the creative well-springs still flowed freely, he had attained the maturity which he now shows! But alas! I noticed in *Aida* an ominous weakening of melodic invention . . .

Verdi himself—that is to say, only the old Verdi —was more tolerant. He alone practised tolerance, because he was a great human being, because he felt artistically sure of himself and perhaps—just a little —by reason of the indifference that comes with age.

All this has not been cited as proof that great musicians are especially unjust or devoid of judgment. If they are, it is a toll which they pay to their greatness. The creative man sits in a cage, wholly preoccupied with himself. He sees with a keen eye, but he is too close for a good view. He is always, or almost always, myopic. His judgment, whether praise or blame, is important and throws light—sometimes on the object of the praise or blame, and always on the great man himself. Objectivity is not permitted to a creator. Only love and hate, and—in a case of complete superiority—loneliness and tolerance.

o II o

To this inability of great men to be just to others, in spite of the uncommon sagacity which none of them lacks, we may perhaps trace the fact that great artists rarely possess the talent to teach—and often have an aversion to teaching. Bach, once again, is an exception. To him music is an art that is practised as a craft, fixed by firm and communicable rules, which accordingly he communicates to his sons and pupils—including a son-in-law. That he was a good teacher is particularly evident from the great independence evinced by Friedemann and Philip Emanuel, his most famous sons. Handel, on the other hand, is again the opposite to Bach in that he keeps an amanuensis but trains no pupils—

neither young professionals nor 'ladies and gentlemen' who presumably would have paid him high
fees. He does not bother with that. And Gluck? We
know full well that a pretty obscure musician, one
Karl Hanke, has boasted of his lessons with Gluck,
but they seem to have consisted only in his being
admitted to the house to listen to the performances
of Gluck's niece and in his receiving occasional bits
of advice—like the favorite Salieri. There was, indeed, a progeny of Gluckists in the field of opera,
but there were no Gluck pupils.

Mozart gave lessons—in piano playing, in composition, and with more or less repugnance, according to the qualities of the pupil; but never with
pleasure. His description of how he wanted to make
the sluggish arteries of the young Duchesse de
Guines pulsate more amply constitutes one of the
most drastic and tragi-comic pages in his correspondence. But also in his relation to more highly gifted
pupils, such as Stephen Storace, Thomas Attwood,
and Johann Nepomuk Hummel, there seems to be
more of kind-heartedness than joy in teaching. The
exercise books that have been preserved, for instance
Attwood's, prove that he was not nearly so strict
with his pupils as others had been with him and as

he was with himself. From Beethoven's dissatisfaction with Haydn we may conclude that the latter was a bad teacher—certainly a much worse one than Albrechtsberger. And that Beethoven himself was a dangerous one, in the rare cases in which he accepted a pupil, or was forced to accept one—for instance the Archduke Rudolph—we see from the compositions of his pupil and compatriot Ferdinand Ries. For Ries learned from Beethoven only his reckless and improvisional manner but no discipline in the larger forms, and no craftsmanship in detail. And Schubert? He died too young, and imagined himself to be still a learner; so he hardly felt able or willing to function as a teacher.

Schumann established golden rules for the learner; but he had no pupils in the true sense. Mendelssohn, as we have seen, was a bad conservatory director. He was just as 'finished' and superior as Mozart, but he lacked Mozart's patience and goodness of heart. Chopin was a piano teacher, and accepted this profession because he had to; but one reads only too easily between the lines when he reports dryly to his relatives, on 18 April 1847: 'Yesterday I had to give seven lessons, and to people who are soon to depart.' His inimitable yet a thousand-fold imitated art he could not teach to anybody.

Wagner was 'the master,' with a troop of disciples but no pupils. It is as impossible to imagine him correcting school papers as it is to imagine Verdi doing anything of the kind. Nevertheless he did give his disciple Bülow a few priceless hints, as the man of experience to the novice—hints which Bülow, with his infinite cleverness, could have made use of, too, if he had possessed a stronger creative faculty. Liszt was no composition teacher, because he had nothing to communicate in the way of craftsmanship. His pianistic teaching activity was the generosity of the *grandseigneur,* and as such was shamelessly abused. Nobody really learned from Liszt, the pianist; and the older generation of today still remembers with horror the 'inspired' and 'temperamental' playing of the immeasurable horde of male and female pianists who boasted of being pupils of Liszt. Brahms' sparse pedagogy (his only reputed pupil was Gustav Jenner, later on the musical director of the University of Marburg) consisted of pointing to the greatness and virtue of the pre-classics and classics.

A great man is not very suited to insinuating himself into the being and growing of another—

and all the less so when the other is himself a person of character. Today, after the romantic individualism of the Wagner and post-Wagner periods, teaching has become possible once more—say, with composers like Hindemith or Křenek—and in the case of the best it has even become a pleasure. But that is because it has once again become an objective and generally communicable handicraft, a technique (say, in the use of the twelve-tone system), as it was in the sixteenth and seventeenth centuries.

IV

Historical Conditions for Greatness

Here is a hero who has done nought but shake the tree,
when the fruit is ripe. Do you think this too little? Then
look first upon the tree which he has shaken.

NIETZSCHE: *The Wanderer and
his Shadow*, Aphorism 347.

$\mathcal{G}$REATNESS is possible in every stage of development in art. But lasting, 'eternal' greatness is possible only when an abnormal force—a genius—coincides with the right moment in the development of art, as it has been expressed by Jacob Burckhardt, to whom this book owes so much.

There are happy and unhappy periods for artists in general, and for great artists in particular; and the 'immortal' artists have shown their genius, as it were, also in this—to have been born at the right moment. In a more primitive stage of art-development there are no 'unhappy' periods. They occur only after those 'revolutions' of which, as we know, musical history records several—the periods when, following a climax, there has been a decline, and a new and painful ascent must be begun. The first of these 'revolutions' may be fixed at about 1520; and it may well be that before this time, too, there were variations in the tempo of development, quieter moments alternating with more agitated ones in the progress of art, but not really unfavorable ones. What did not happen, for instance, in that earlier time, is that a nation persisted, through pride and conservatism, in an older tradition until it was overrun and overwhelmed by a foreign nation's art, which in the meantime had progressed at dizzying speed—as was the case of England in Corelli's and Handel's time. There were, it is true, national differences in the Middle Ages, but they were merely variants of a universal art, in the course of which some nation—the French, the English, the Burgundian—occupied the foreground, as the leader. What has been called the Florentine art of the *trecento,* or the 'Italian pre-renaissance,' is not a 'renaissance,' since there was nothing to be 're-born'; it was only a particularly fresh and enchanting blossom on the bush of medieval art, which was essentially French. 'Pre-Renaissance' is a particularly unhappy and misleading designation, for Italian art of the fourteenth century is an afterglow rather than a period before the dawn. In the fifteenth century, when this 'pre-renaissance' was over, Italy submit-

ted willingly to the importation of so-called French-
Burgundian art music, represented most brilliantly
by the name of Guillaume Dufay. Italy did not
begin to develop its own modest national art until
the end of the century.

○ 2 ○

IN the Middle Ages the relationship of the 'artist'—
if this designation is at all permissible—was never
antagonistic to the time, a circumstance which we
shall have to treat more particularly later on. The
'artist' was the architect, the sculptor, the painter,
the poet, the musician who knew his trade, and if
he was very proficient in it he might perhaps rise
above anonymity. The fact that artists organized
themselves in guilds—for the purposes of their art,
not for purely social and economic ends, as today—
is significant enough. What happened in music was
essentially the same as what happened in painting.
Duccio da Buoninsegna, of Siena, distinguished
himself in the Byzantine tradition—a universal, international tradition in those days—without breaking it in any way. In Florence (which already in the
thirteenth century had a *vicolo dei pittori*—a 'Street

of the Painters') Cimabue 'revived' the decayed and obsolete Byzantine forms; and this revival is a process so mysterious as to defy explanation, for it is no explanation—merely a parallel—to associate it with the awakening of a new religious experience and the name of St. Francis of Assisi. Giotto, the pupil of Cimabue, then dispensed with the Byzantine tradition altogether, but not by conscious opposition to it: indeed, if one had called him a revolutionary, he would have expressed both astonishment and resentment. What he created became the basis of a new tradition and the starting point for other painters and pupils; and this continuous progression gave to the history of medieval art its logic and its certainty —a history which found its most reliable documentation in the art works themselves, and not in letters and archives.

It is no different in any other field of art. François Villon was a rogue, but not a revolutionary; he wrote rebellious stuff, but wrote it while anxiously clinging to traditional form. Similarly, the roving minstrels of the Middle Ages may have been vagabonds with a touch of genius; in any case they were vagabonds, who found the guild beyond their reach. Leoninus and Perotinus, two highly esteemed masters of the guild in Paris, have survived in musical history; and Guillaume Dufay was the first master of his time because he was more proficient in his craft than anyone else. Quite like his contemporary Donatello, the ironmolder and sculptor, who presumably never had the feeling of being an 'artist.'

In the sixteenth century the musician is already a 'lonely' man; the world concedes him a greater right, a greater freedom to rise above the common stream—yes, even to alter the course of the stream —but not to swim against it. However, about this power to alter the course of the stream we shall speak a little later. The revolution in the first quarter of the sixteenth century was of the rarer kind which so to speak takes place beneath the surface of the stream—without manifestos and proclamations, even though it was not entirely unnoticed. It was certainly noticed by the printer Francesco Marcolini in Venice, who in 1536 declares Josquin's whole generation, including the great master himself, to be outmoded and superseded. There were in those times more progressive artists, as well as some who were more loyal to tradition; but no sharp conflict resulted. Indeed, there were masters who united progress and tradition in their person, who followed sometimes one tendency and sometimes the other, without obstructing either. But the condition of music about 1600 was such that for the people of the time it was either completely dead or completely alive. It was a book with seven seals to those who understand music only when it is a clear image of an animated passion—which is just what music became about A.D. 1600. To him who possesses the key, it opens a world of purer and more naive symbolism; and he finds it rather less than perfect whenever it is obscured by a striving for emotion, expression or delineation. But stylistically it is perfect within itself. The sixteenth century was a 'happy' time for music; the *Missa Papæ Marcelli* is, to us, as well-rounded, self-contained a work as it was about 1560.

° 3 °

WITH the opening of the new century—the seventeenth—there begins a less favorable era in music, seen from the point of view of 'eternity,' of the durability of the works which were produced. All these cantatas, arias, operas, oratorios, all these *canzone,* sonatas, fantasias, and concertos, are in the nature of experiments. They are degrees in the de-

velopment of music, not perfection; they point forward, without being that which is complete in
itself. Greatness is definitely possible in such a
period. Indeed, it is perhaps a twofold greatness—
a tragic greatness, if one considers what the struggle
for the attainment of an ideal really is—a *heroic*
fight.

One of the victims of this time of transition is
Monteverdi. Monteverdi was the great experimen-
ter, who in the course of his experiments in musical
chemistry smashed many phials and retorts without
producing genuine gold: ore which contains gold,
yes, but not pure gold. The madrigals which he
wrote no longer appealed to the cheerful and established musical society of the time of Giovanni Gabrieli, or Orazio Vecchi, but only to a small, unstable
circle of aristocratic connoisseurs who took pleasure
in experiments as such. His monodies are 'programmatic,' his duets are dry and primitive. His operas,
of which we know only those of his last period, be-
tray his starting point—intuitive genius, i.e. *Orfeo*
—also his incipient conventionality, i.e. *L'Incoronazione di Poppea*. And this conventionality is still
blended with the old personal, revolutionary genius
of the master. Everywhere the great personality of

(203)

Monteverdi lights up, with increasing brilliance, the wildness of this baroque work of dissolution and construction. Yet his immortality is historical rather than real. He can no longer be made to live, as Bach was made to live again a century ago, or as Mozart could always be made to live again, if ever his works should be temporarily lost.

A German example of greatness in a musically unhappy period is Heinrich Schütz. Here was a musician distinguished for the power and depth of his feeling, for the keenness of his observation, and the universality of his intellect; for his power and fantasy in handling the language: a master whose life fell between two periods of development, when the old forms of the so-called 'a-cappella music' had become archaic, and the new revolutionary forms of the seventeenth century were still unready, still in the full flux of creation. He felt the danger of the unreadiness of the new, and sometimes he returned to the style of the time of Palestrina—without, however, being able to secure a greater life to his works in this style than to his attempts in the latest Italian style—the style of writing for a small number of parts with figured bass. When he died, at an advanced age, he was highly esteemed, but without influence. Bach was born only thirteen years after Schütz's death; but there is no longer any visible bridge that leads from the work of Heinrich Schütz to that of Johann Sebastian Bach. To call Schütz a 'forerunner' of Bach is a mere convention; the forms which Bach inherited are earlier, or later, more finished forms. And after that, Schütz was forgotten until the scholarship of the nineteenth century bethought itself of him in loving remembrance, but without being able to revive him. Whenever one of his curious Passions is performed, the effect is always the same: a few experts are astonished and delighted; the general public finds the music strange. And then—a further slumber in the treasure chest of the past. Unhappy greatness!

The English victim of the 'unreadiness' of the seventeenth century is Henry Purcell. His early death has justly been called not only a personal tragedy but a national misfortune. He wrote, when still a youth, a number of—as it were—'posthumous' pieces for string instruments, in a style corresponding to the 'fancy' of the seventeenth century, that is, without use of the figured bass; and these are perhaps the most finished, the most enduring, the most 'eternal' things in the many volumes of his

Complete Works. For the figured bass, in the music of the seventeenth century, is the vehicle of improvisation, and thereby becomes an obstacle to the organic development of a musical work of art. The most enduring works of the seventeenth century are those in which the *basso continuo* plays quite a minor role, or no role at all—the *ricercari* and fugues and fantasies of the great organ and harpsichord masters, and the trio-sonatas for two violins, violoncello and bass, in which all voices are vital and organic. In the cases of musicians like Frescobaldi in Rome, Buxtehude in Lübeck, Lübeck in Hamburg, it is remarkable how feeble their vocal works are in comparison with their instrumental fantasies and fugues. Well, what Purcell wrote in the way of sacred and secular vocal music is perhaps the most perfect music in the 'concerted' style that could be written about 1690: solo passages alternating with choir, and human voices with instruments, with magnificently long-breathed melodies over an *ostinato* bass or 'ground.'

Purcell is the consummation of the English tradition over half a century. But this art was too definitely a tradition, with its mixture of popularly facile invention and popularly facile texture. In the meantime a few Italian masters—Carissimi and his disciples in vocal music, Torelli and Corelli and their forerunners in instrumental music—had created a more sophisticated and sensuous style of melody, as well as stricter and simpler forms. Purcell was enraptured by this art; he wanted to transplant it to England, as is shown in the foreword to his *Sonatas of III Parts* of 1683. 'The author . . . ,' he says, 'is not asham'd to own his unskilfulness in the Italian Language; but that's the unhappiness of his Education, which cannot justly be accounted his fault, however he thinks he may warrantly affirm, that he is not mistaken in the power of the Italian Notes, or elegancy of their compositions, which he would recommend to English Artists . . .' And so he composes his trio-sonatas, which in their mixture of southern and northern, conventional and individual elements, are more attractive than anything created in Italy at this time. But it was too late. After him there appeared a great genius of Italian stamp, together with the ready forms which then were new for England but already classical in Italy; in other words, victorious, incontestable, and sensually convincing. After that, for a time, there was an end of English music.

(207)

° 4 °

ALL this is not to minimize what charm the 'unready' work, the work of periods which we have
called 'unhappy,' can exercise—especially on times
like our own, which are themselves in the stage of
experimentation, transition, and unreadiness. Here
the law of attraction and repulsion, or what we have
called the law of the affinity of periods, plays its
part. 'Romantic' times are attracted by the romantic; 'classical' times by the classical. One period appreciates the sketch more than the finished product;
and a time like ours, which would like so much to
negate all tradition, and which would most like to
begin from the beginning, cultivates a strange relationship to all that is primitive, exotic—yes, even
barbaric. The same process is reflected in all the arts.
The nineteenth century rediscovered Gothic art; and
it is due only to the slower tempo of scientific research in music that the musical Middle Ages were
not rediscovered until the end of the nineteenth
century. John Ruskin saw in the renaissance a symp-
tom of decadence; for several decades the Pre-Raphaelites preferred the *quattrocento* to the mature

art of the *cinquecento*. Indeed, in Central Europe, a celebrated Swiss art historian, Heinrich Woelfflin, had to undertake to 'save' Leonardo da Vinci, Raphael, and Michelangelo from neglect. It is not mere disguised nationalism that places Purcell higher than Handel; it is not mere snobbery when some eccentrics love Heinrich Schütz more deeply than Bach; and it is not mere aversion to the internationally popular Italy of the nineteenth century when the younger musicians of Italy say that Monteverdi means much more to them than Verdi—or, save the mark!—Puccini. The historical evaluation of preparatory and classical periods, the 'happy' and 'unhappy' times, will always vary in accordance with ever-changing 'affinity' to an ever-changing present.

∘ 5 ∘

ENDURING greatness—'happiness' in greatness— is not possible without a great heritage, and this heritage must come at the right time, that is, neither too early nor too late. It is of course not necessary to emphasize that this 'happiness' of the historical constellation has nothing to do with personal happiness. We do not know whether that mysterious

(209)

person who bore the name of Handel, of whom there exist only some two dozen letters, with not a single intimate one among them; in whose life women seem to have played no part, and whose character is revealed only in a few silly anecdotes—we do not know whether he was happy or not. Great, and fortunate in his heritage, he certainly was. We do not know whether Bach was happy or unhappy: even in his mundane life he seems to stand above the ordinary concepts of happiness and misfortune. But have we really drawn the correct conclusions from his deep disdain of authority, documented by the occasion, in his youth, on which he overstayed his leave; and from the impishness of his behavior, when he threw the congregation off pitch with his organ-playing; from his irascibility *vis-à-vis* the Leipzig town council? That Mozart was not a happy person we know from a hundred anecdotes, and from a hundred passages in his letters; and we probably know less from what they contain than from what they omit. He was not quite equal to life at any time; and in this he is the antithesis of that other 'Knight of the Golden Spur,' Christoph Willibald Ritter von Gluck, who was equal to all the exigencies of life. But, by way of compensation, Gluck must have been conscious of another shortcoming—in his creative ability—especially when, near the end of his life, he heard the *Entführung* of his younger colleague. This brings us to the true distinctions. Let a person's individual happiness be what it may: the happiness of perfecting a form which has reached completion, or of bringing to completion one which is all but complete—that happiness a creator alone can know; it fills his whole being and is not to be compared with any happiness on earth. This happiness is one which *must* coincide with that 'happy' turn of history, which is the subject of our discourse.

This historical good fortune is of course worthless, without the 'abnormal force' to exploit it. Thousands of talented people live through it without knowing or feeling that it exists. Perhaps they are just the people who profit from the situation, like Telemann, Bach's more famous contemporary, who fused Italian, German, and French ingredients into a highly agreeable and amiable synthesis. Handel, the 'Italian,' was much more one-sided than Telemann—and much greater. And Bach did something quite different: he was much more the true *heir* than Telemann, and what he produced was much more than a mere synthesis. Indeed, he was not only an heir, but a revolutionary as well. Revolutionary not in the banal sense of the destroyer of ancient forms, but as the re-interpreter of these forms—their 'fulfiller,' who fills them with new meaning—a process of development for which the word 'evolution' is not quite adequate. It goes far beyond mere 'completion' or consummation. Indeed, a choral fantasy by Bach differs from those of his predecessors, or progenitors, only in its musical power; a fugue only in the strength of character of his theme and its development. But nothing like his 'Inventions' and 'Symphonies,' this union of education and art in the very highest sense, had ever been seen. Here was something which, in Bach's time, at least, simply did not exist. Perhaps it would be more correct to say that it had ceased to exist, since something similar had been produced by the earlier Italians, who wrote 'duos,' by way of études and vocalises. That, for the historian, is the astonishing thing about Bach—how deeply his roots reach into the soil of the past. He is the perfector and consummator, not of an epoch but of several centuries. When at the end of his life Bach wrote his *Musicalische Opfer* and his *Art of Fugue,* he lived spiritually, musically, no longer in his time but in an earlier century, when musicians still wrote *ricercari,* and understood the art of thematic transformation in a higher sense than that of the variation. For this *Opfer* and this *Art of Fugue,* with their supernatural vitality, have only an external similarity to the mathematical-contrapuntal diversions which the seventeenth and eighteenth century preferred: here Bach reaches across these centuries into remoter times, when polyphony had not yet degenerated into a state of torpidity, as it had in his own time.

Nothing in Bach is unready, or does it point to the future; in everything he touched he said the last word. In the proper sense no fugues were written after Bach; actually, indeed very many more fugues were written, but none that went beyond the established requirements of the form. They merely filled out the form. Mozart's fugues are all anachronisms; they are perhaps his only unhappy, uncomfortable, if not unaccomplished works. Beethoven's fugues are not fugues, not self-contained artistic images, but sections of movements which are used for something within the frame-work of the sonata. Technically, Brahms would probably

(213)

have been capable of writing a Bachian fugue, but he refrained. Or rather, he wrote fugues only as exercises. Fugues are still written today for pedagogical purposes; and perhaps also fugues for artistic uses, in 'modernistic' music. But they are—and want to be—something different from a Bach fugue.

The same 'conclusive' attribute applies to Bach's concerto, and to Bach's monumental, static aria. As a composer of concertos Bach was an imitator of Vivaldi; but Vivaldi is far more modern than his great imitator, and projects more threads into the future. The Bachian aria, inwardly emotional, is fully contained within itself, like a jewel in a necklace. And whichever of Bach's forms one may examine, it always points to the past, never to the future. He uses Italian and French suggestions, but does not use Italian or French music. His historical 'happiness' is, if you will, very egoistic. But just because he has said the last word for his time, he has said it perhaps for all time. With him we enter into a closed-off world, which is perfect in itself, stylistically pure, and therefore beautiful. He is, among all great musicians, the most enduring.

There is another sign to indicate the historical position of Johann Sebastian Bach: he was the last *painter* in music, despite Schubert and Berlioz, and in this, too, he is the heir of a two-centuries-old tradition. From 1530 onward the general tendency of all vocal music, and of some instrumental music, was to 'paint' the word, the sense of the word, in music, to illustrate it in tones. The great esthetic slogan of the time was *'imitatio naturæ.'* The means of 'imitating nature' are without number. In part they are symbolical, in part realistic; and sometimes they are very naive. One might compile a table of such means of rendering tangible concepts like day and night, sweetness and bitterness, calm and movement; it would be a contribution to the history of the baroque in music. The seventeenth century altered nothing in this esthetic tendency; on the contrary, it intensified it. One need only examine a recitative of Carissimi or Agostino Steffani in order to realize that the old masters were not concerned with feeling, but with delineation, with a drastic materialization of the word, with symbols. All that was taken over by Bach. I am convinced— let it be said once again—that we put much too much emotion or expression into his language where it is intended to be purely descriptive or symbolical, and, in fact, have not even yet recognized many of

Bach's musical symbols. Only after his time did the reign of emotional music, of musical sentimentality, begin.

At the cost of being un-chronological (but chronology does not matter in this book) we may at this point mention Palestrina as being most eminently an heir—an heir in an even purer sense than Bach—or at least in a different sense. Palestrina owes his semi-legendary position in musical history very largely to his attribute as an heir. He persisted in his heritage, although his period was already beginning to pass beyond him, although it was not yet conscious of its revolutionary powers. Between 1550 and 1590, there were, besides Palestrina, a number of Netherlanders and Italian masters with far stronger personalities than his, but without the heritage of so much past; or who, like the Venetian Andrea Gabrieli, already stood much more definitely between conservatism and progress. Palestrina, the Roman, had much more 'tradition' in him than this or that Netherlander or compatriot—people who already pointed the way into the seventeenth century. Palestrina embodies only the sixteenth; he is a traditionalist, and so he is capable of perfecting what we call the a-cappella style with greater purity in contour and color than any contemporary. He is not only a traditionalist, but a reactionary—and not alone in the field of the madrigal (in which he follows the bolder contemporary rather haltingly, some twenty years behind), but in the Mass. Also, he shows a violent aversion to many of his younger contemporaries. But within his own enclosure he attains the ideal, and his greatness remains undisputed, as indeed it should.

o 6 o

IN this connection let it be said, about the fortunes of art in general and those of music in particular, that here, in contradistinction to science, the question of priority is of no importance whatever. In music the important thing is not so much to invent something as to execute it. Musical histories make a great deal of fuss about Monteverdi having been the first to use the unprepared seventh; but it would not detract in the least from his greatness if we were to show that the unprepared seventh had already occurred before his time, for instance in the music of Gesualdo. It has often been pointed out that the chromatic suspensions of *Tristan* were

GREATNESS IN MUSIC

prominently anticipated by Louis Spohr, the chromaticist *par excellence* of his time; indeed, one may find the same device in Mozart, namely in the slow movement of the E-flat major string quartet. (Wagner knew Spohr very well, and even treated him in quite a friendly fashion, since Spohr had said friendly things about *The Flying Dutchman* and *Tannhäuser*). Nevertheless the opening bars of *Tristan* remain what they are—the revelation of a new world of harmony and emotion. In science an accidental lucky find may be of great importance; in science a young Saul may set forth to retrieve his father's ass and and find a kingdom. In music, 'getting an idea' means little; molding the idea—giving it form—is everything. Of course one must have, or find, the right ideas—the ideas suitable to the work to be formed. And the quality of these ideas constitutes a *difference* between one creative musician and another; but not an *antithesis*—not the difference between good and bad.

In the case of Beethoven this process of formation can, thanks to his sketch books, be followed with better documentary support than with other masters—masters who created under different conditions. For instance, Mozart and Schubert, because

they were more definitely *heirs:* Mozart the heir of
the eighteenth century, of Johann Christian Bach,
of Haydn and Johann Sebastian Bach; Schubert the
heir of Mozart, Rossini, and, above all, of Beethoven. But even Mozart did not work differently
from Beethoven; or from the poet Schiller, who
approached the task of creating a poem in a sort of
musical mood—a premonition of the impression
which the completed work should make upon the
recipient. Nor, again, was Mozart's method very
different from that of a mathematical genius like
Karl Friedrich Gauss, who once remarked: 'I have
been sure of my results for some time; what I don't
know is how I shall arrive at them.' In the same way
Beethoven had long 'been sure of his results,' but
it cost him labor to arrive at them. But it would be
wrong to believe that these results were in the nature of some non-musical 'idea,' some poetic 'program.' They were music, and nothing else.

As has just been indicated, Mozart was another
of the great ones whom history designated to say
the last word. Just because he stood at the end of
an epoch and not at the beginning—though no
musician of course stands *wholly* at an end or *wholly*
at a beginning—he may perhaps be destined to

reach further into the future than Beethoven. Beethoven was quite differently constituted; he was just as great as Mozart, but he stood more at a beginning than at an end. Mozart may well have come into the world at a dangerous moment of musical history—six years after the death of Bach, whose figure protruded like that of a contrapuntal fossil into a period of music that had become *galant* —that is, in a time which no longer recognized anything but the light, the playful, the Anacreontic and the superficial, a time whose idol was Pergolesi. Indeed, only a few old pedants and scholars like that severe gentleman, J. N. Forkel, Bach's first biographer, despised and execrated Pergolesi and everything Pergolesian.

Mozart's musical education was very characteristic. It was almost completely Italian, in other words 'galant'; and it would have produced works of the empty gracefulness of—say, Boccherini, if in early youth he had not had the good fortune to fall into the hands of Johann Christian Bach, the youngest son of the great Sebastian, also known as the 'Milan' or the 'London' Bach. Among Mozart's many models, Johann Christian Bach was the one from whom he derived his warmth of heart and his

(220)

melodic simplicity. He could, however, not have acquired them if they had not already been present within him. But in his youth Mozart, like Johann Christian Bach himself, often forgot this simplicity and sailed in the shallow waters of the 'galant'—the merely polite. That is the one side of Mozart's apprenticeship; the other is the crudest and driest counterpoint, the starkest pedantry, which was possible only in a period which no longer had any conception of live, vital polyphony. With this sort of counterpoint young Mozart properly tormented himself—in Bologna under Padre Martini, the musical oracle of his time; then in Salzburg, where he filled one exercise book after another with copies of archaic church compositions by Michael Haydn and Daniel Eberlin. This irreconcilable contradiction and break in style constituted a rift in his creation throughout this time, and it increased to the danger point when, about 1782, in his first Vienna year, he got to know works of genuine, vital polyphony like the *Well-tempered Clavichord,* the organ trios, and even the *Art of Fugue* of Johann Sebastian Bach.

But he was lucky. For he had, in Joseph Haydn, an older colleague who experienced the same conflict in his creative work. Haydn, too, began as a 'galant' composer; he, too, in his quartets and symphonies, felt that **counterpoint** and 'learnèd' polyphony were foreign bodies in his style. He, too, felt the weakness of the merely 'polite' style, and therefore wrote quartets with fugues for his *finali*, and symphonies with canonic minuets. Finally, at the age of fifty, he found the solution. He wrote quartets which are neither 'galant' nor learned, but both in one—quartets with 'thematic development,' quartets in which every voice is an obbligato part, or, as the Parisians so aptly called them, *quatuors dialogués*. After he found that solution, Haydn wrote no more fugues. He did not, however, throw strict counterpoint overboard; but now it became the butt of his humor, his whimsicality, his irony.

Mozart did not follow him that far. To him counterpoint in all its forms, as an element of music, was too serious a matter. After becoming acquainted with the works of Johann Sebastian Bach, in 1782 and 1783, he wrote some very unpleasing, strained, antiquated fugues. Later he no longer did anything of the sort. But never again did he dispense with polyphony, nor did he write counterpoint just for fun, like Haydn. Mozart dissolved counterpoint in his own style. He dissolved it in such a way that one is no longer conscious of it. Who can tell whether the minuets in the G-minor quintet, in the E-flat major piano trio (with clarinet) or the G-minor symphony were written in the 'galant' or the 'learnèd' style? Not in the conventional 'learnèd' style, to be sure; yet in a 'strict' and genuine polyphony, though we are hardly aware of it: in the minuet of the symphony not until the trio has flitted by. Is the slow movement of the C-major string quartet 'galant' or 'learnèd'? The 'reality,' i.e. the independence, of the four parts could not be more pronounced, and the concluding melody of the first violin in the Coda is the most beautiful and most noble counterpoint in the world. Thirty or forty years after the death of Bach, Mozart, with the help of Haydn, overcame a crisis in the history of music. His work is a conclusion—a final word. Haydn did not go beyond Mozart; he only adopted from him a new cantabile style, a new sweetness of melody.

Another 'last word' was said in Mozart's piano concertos. In this field, too, he completed the whole cycle of development in the span of a few years. The piano concerto was still young in Mozart's time. It had its point of departure not, of course, in the concertos of Bach, but in the works of several Germans, Frenchmen, and Poles, such as Schobert, Raupach, and, above all, Johann Salomon Schroeter and Johann Christian Bach. And before Mozart it was a comparatively primitive structure, in which the piano dominated, and only a loose relationship existed between *tutti* and *soli*. In Mozart's piano concerto we see the culmination not only of his own symphonic creation—a risky thing to say to any-one who appreciates the Prague Symphony and the G-minor, E-flat and C-major symphonies—but of the entire species. Here has been attained a perfec-tion in which everything is balanced to a hair—art as against 'entertainment'; contrasting of two sonor-ities as against blending them: here we have the perfect equilibrium between the symphonic and the *concertante* styles. Already Beethoven had to shift this balance in favor of the 'dramatic,' in favor of the competition between solo and orchestra—both in response to his temperament and in accordance with the development of the species, which would brook no standing still, no mere repetition. But Mozart's piano concerto is one of the most wonder-

ful examples of the 'happy historical moment' coin-
ciding with the 'abnormal force.'

Yet another example is Mozart's *opera buffa,* as
exemplified in *Nozze di Figaro, Don Giovanni,* and
Così fan tutte. These are the apex of their species,
and an apex which surmounts all national divisions.
True, there are Rossini's *Barber,* Donizetti's *Don
Pasquale,* and Verdi's *Falstaff.* Here we have three
works which are much more 'buffo' than *Nozze di
Figaro,* more even than the most farcical of Mozart's three—*Così fan tutte.* (*Don Giovanni,* which
is incommensurable, may be left out of this comparison.) The *Barbiere di Siviglia* is the Italian ideal
of the species, *Falstaff* a late return to this ideal—at
once a looking backward to a brilliantly happy national past and a pointing forward to a future yet
unknown. But *Figaro* is *opera buffa,* and more: it
is *opera buffa* in some of its traditional figures, like
Bartolo and Marcellina; and it is musical comedy,
reaching out towards the eternal regions of the
human drama, in such characters as Cherubino, the
Count and Countess, Susanna and Figaro. The
limits of the species are preserved, and yet exceeded,
in a mysterious and imperceptible way. Verdi, too,
exceeded the boundaries in *Falstaff.* Indeed, the

(225)

scene in which Master Ford feels the horns growing on his head—

È sogno o realtà? . . .

is not merely comic, but tragic—more than anything a counterpart to Iago's 'Credo.' Rossini jokes about his characters, who are as unreal as marionettes. Verdi's characters are by no means marionettes; although their creator does not love them— being too old for that. He has made them and he observes them, in their ludicrous and futile behavior as well as in their narrowness and wickedness —like a demigod who has ceased to be touched by anything that happens on this earth.

Who would determine whether Mozart's *Figaro* is 'German' or 'Italian'? Investigations of that sort are no longer undertaken except by musico-historical 'racial experts.' The answer is: they are Mozartian. Here perhaps one should emphasize once again that the concept 'national music' does not imply areas confined within already existing boundaries, or enclosures, into which the masters allow themselves to be marched, like recruits under the drill sergeant's command. These areas are *created* only by the masters themselves. There is such a thing as French music because there is a Lully, Rameau, Couperin, Berlioz, and Debussy. There is Italian music not because there were and are Neapolitan street singers and Venetian *gondolieri,* but because there were and are composers like Monteverdi, Carissimi, Pergolesi, and Domenico Scarlatti. German music? German music is Bach, Haydn, Mozart, Beethoven; and even they are not easily brought under one roof. This Germanism is, thank God, not the political Germanism which came into existence some time after the Napoleonic wars, but an ideal Germanism which not even this political Germanism could affect—or can or ever will affect, through all the ages to come.

One of the most striking and in the truest sense wonderful examples of greatness in a happy historical constellation—the meeting of genius with favorable historical development—is Schubert. His poor, restricted personal life was anything but happy. There is nothing more heart-rending than to follow the life story of this assistant teacher of Lichtenthal, who, having been scantily fed through life by his friends, proceeded from disappointment to disappointment, and died at the age of thirty-two from a seemingly absurd disease. But when he wrote his

(227)

sonatas, trios, quartets, symphonies, masses, choruses, and songs, he must have experienced not only
the happiness of creating, but also the miracle of
being able to create so easily. This effortless creation, this wealth of creative capacity, and the immeasurable abundance of his heritage were the result
of a unique constellation in the history of music,
plus a unique gift. The gift is incommensurable,
but the constellation can be described. It is musical
history's lucky throw. Schubert lived in the shadows
of Haydn, of Mozart (whose real influence became
effective only about 1800), and of Beethoven; and
Beethoven's greatness alone would have crushed
every other contemporary capable of measuring it.
Schubert was great enough to write, in Beethoven's
lifetime, or about the year of his death, the 'finished Unfinished' and the C-major symphony, the
quartets in A minor and D minor, and the first movement of the G-major quartet, in which the whole of
Bruckner, and more than Bruckner, is already contained. He knew how to inherit—all of Mozart, as
much of Haydn as he could use—and he knew how
to appropriate not only the melodic treasures of
Hungary and Upper Austria and whatever funda-
mental melody the Vienna of 1800-1825 might

have brought to him, but also Rossini, or as much of him as found useful. No other composer of instrumental music exploited the situation as Schubert did. The question whether he belongs to the eighteenth or nineteenth century has never yet been posed, and it is futile to discuss it now. His life was too short, his appearance too divine—too heavenly —to permit of any classification. If Goethe could have had any degree of knowledge of Schubert's greatness, he might rather have symbolized him than Byron—and with far more justification—in the figure of his Euphorion; for Byron lacked precisely the essential quality of Euphorion—the purity, the childlikeness in his maturity, the maturity in his childlikeness.

The purest outcome of the happy constellation is Schubert's *Lied*. Here three things came together: the development of the species, the development of German poetry and—Schubert's gift. For all his talent Schubert, had he been born thirty years earlier, could no more have brought the species to its climax than Haydn and Mozart were able to do; although the talent was not lacking in either case! Haydn did not compose any text of genuine poetic content at all; Mozart composed only one, quite by accident, namely Goethe's *Veilchen*. And he composed it, not as a song but as a *scena,* somewhat in the Italian style, and—following the old and traditionally sovereign attitude of the musician towards the librettist or purveyor of texts—without genuine respect. In short, Mozart far outweighs Goethe in this song. Haydn's songs mostly got stuck in old-fashioned pedantry, Mozart's in the Anacreontic spirit which was so current in his time. In both cases the musician was the lord and master. With Schubert this false relationship had ceased to exist. In the meantime, thanks to Goethe, a new kind of German poetry had come to flourish—a poetic style no longer epigrammatical or Anacreontic—no longer an exercise of intellect and wit, but a perfect verbal expression of direct human experience. This kind of poetry had also been set to music before Schubert, especially by musicians who were personally close to the circle of Goethe and Schiller—such as Kayser, Reichardt, and Zumsteg. Schubert had known them all, and had followed in their footsteps for a time, especially in those of Zumsteg, the amiable Mozartian. But these musicians, for their own part, had come too early, in that they had not as yet experienced Beethoven, with his richer musicality, his more turbulent emotion. Their *Lieder* are a kind of intensified folksongs, much too simple, with too little attempt at exhausting the content of the poem.

With Schubert all that is brought into balance. No one can say whether the poetry exists for his music, or his music for the poetry. They form a unity. Who could ever again, after Schubert, set to music *Heidenröslein* or *Gretchen am Spinnrad* or *An Schwager Kronos?* Hugo Wolf challenged comparison with Schubert with the settings of some other poems—with *Prometheus* and *Ganymed* and the songs from *Wilhelm Meister;* and in doing so has furnished the most convulsive music among all the convulsive and yet magnificent things he ever wrote. Better and more genuine songs than those of Schubert have never been written and will never be written, because that particular constellation of time and genius will never occur again, nor the combination of youth and maturity which brought them to life.

° 7 °

THERE is the musician who is against his time, and the musician who is with his time. If one speaks of the 'musician against his time' as of one of the great men who have won the world despite its opposition, as of a great conqueror, then Richard Wagner has the greatest claim to the title. But he was not the first. And he is not a pure type of the species—of which a pure type does not, in fact, exist. In some trait of his character even the most determined revolutionary goes along *with* his time; in some other even the most conciliating, most careful genius gives offense to time.

In order to avoid the all-too-historical, we shall not speak of the revolutionaries of earlier times. It is certain that Cipriano de Rore or Claudio Monteverdi were musicians against their time; and both of them experienced plenty of hostility from theorizing colleagues, too. But they did not experience the opposition of that which we call 'the public,' because there was no such thing in their time. And there was no public opinion, organized through the press. People in those days were no less malicious and comfortable than in the nineteenth and twentieth centuries; but the masses followed the judgment of those who set the tone, and they were the aristocracy, which always supported the new, and furthered progress and courage in matters intellectual. One of the most provocative, one of the most 'progressive' musicians of all time, namely the Principe Carlo Gesualdo da Venosa, a harmonist of extreme daring and lawlessness, was left completely in peace by his generation, precisely because he was a prince. A prince could take what liberties he wished, even in music. But we should have to write a history of the music of the sixteenth century to show why and in what manner Rore and Monteverdi stood against this, their century.

One of the great masters against his time was Joseph Haydn. True, that is hard for nineteenth- and twentieth-century people to grasp—for people who originated the ridiculous phrase 'Papa Haydn' and then believed it. The phrase 'Papa Haydn' dates from the time when Haydn had conquered the world, and had become old and childish. In fact, the epithet would be exactly right for 'the Master,' i.e. Wagner, though hardly for the revolutionary, and the creator of *Tristan*—only for the head of the house Wahnfried and the husband of Cosima.

Haydn was one of the great men against their time, because he was a 'plebeian.' For his time was a conventional time, and knew no other music than stylized music. Bach's music, and in a different way

Handel's, too, is stylized in a high degree. Bach, in any case, stands above the question of style or non-style, since he could only speak his own language; and Handel, who always wrote for an audience, represents the highest fulfilment of the Italian style, without overstepping its frame by as much as a hair's breadth. But the real revolutionary of the eighteenth century was Haydn, and not Gluck, who only put on the airs of a revolutionary. Gluck broke with some obvious opera conventions in an obvious way; but by no means did he revolutionize the opera. He reformed it, that is, he brought it back to the ideals of simplicity—the same ideals which the Florentine *camerata* espoused two centuries before. *Orfeo, Alceste, Paride ed Elena* are very Italian operas and the two *Iphigenias* very French.

Haydn offended against the style, the sacred conventions of music, in that he made music, so to say, in his shirt-sleeves. He introduced into music the unadorned—not transformed but un-formed music of the lowest classes. It is about as though Richard Strauss today were to introduce into an opera entitled *Montezuma* a genuine Indian melody, a cry of nature, which is contrary to our tonal system. Not *quite* like that, for Haydn did not *quote,* he spoke the 'plebeian' accent as his mother-tongue. He deeply outraged the gentry. For this we have a classic bit of testimony in an article on Haydn by the lexicographer E. L. Gerber. Gerber, who was Haydn's junior by only fourteen years, was a direct eye- and ear-witness of what happened. 'Already his first Quatros,' he writes, 'which became known about the year 1760, created a general sensation. People laughed and were amused, in some quarters, by the extraordinary naïveté and liveliness which was in them, while in other places people shouted about the degradation of music for the sake of tomfoolery, also about outrageous octaves . . .' Haydn, as the first, no longer wrote music that was socially limited. In Berlin, where people were most violently indignant about him, he would not have been able to do this; but obviously it *was* possible in the seclusion of Count Morzin's castle, and even more so in the seclusion of Eisenstadt. Here he could afford to 'become original.' All that was necessary was to please his Prince, and in this he evidently succeeded. The mystery of this Prince, Paul Anton Esterházy, has not yet been solved: he must have taken a secret or unabashed pleasure in the 'jests' of his *Capellmeister,* otherwise he would have dismissed him; or else he simply did not notice anything. However, as late as the seventeen-eighties Emperor Joseph II still called Haydn a *Spassmacher* —a jester—and he never took him into his service.

A true biography of Haydn should be written around his very gradual, slow conquest of his time. Paris and London knew about him before Vienna, and especially before Berlin, which with all its caustic cleverness was without intuition and merely 'intelligent.' And Haydn knew all about that. He found it easy to acknowledge Mozart's genius, because Mozart belonged to a quite different world from his. To use a religious simile, Mozart and Boccherini were doubtless very different in the degree and nature of their gifts, but for all their difference they belonged to the same musical faith, the Catholic musical faith. Haydn, however, was a heretic, and sometimes even a pagan. Mozart was a man of convention. Mozart had, as it were, only educational experiences in music. He never tore down a barrier; it was his privilege to say the deepest, the most profound things in a given frame. What he said with reference to his composition of *Entführung* is valid for his entire creative work: ". . . as passions, whether violent or not, must never be expressed in such a way as to excite disgust, and as music, even in the most terrible situations, must never offend the ear, but must please the hearer, in other words must never cease to be music . . .'* Mozart's music is not popular, nor was it music with a popular appeal; it is suspended in an aristocratic sphere, whence it may occasionally descended to the robuster, jollier regions, to the Salzburgian or the Viennese, as a cherub descends in order to mix with the daughters of the land. Haydn is a stranger to this gentility; he relied upon the truthfulness of his merry and unequivocal temperament. Taine said about Rousseau that he had shown the sunrise to people who had never before left their beds before noon. The same might be said of Haydn. In Jean-Jacques Rousseau's time, which preached a sentimental return to nature, Haydn was already quite nonchalantly sitting in this Paradise, without being aware of it. And his contemporaries laughed, or were indignant about it—until they followed him.

We can easily understand why Beethoven became much more a successor of Haydn than Mozart did—quite aside from the fact that Haydn, like

* From transl. of letter by Emily Anderson.

Beethoven, was essentially an instrumental composer; though both wrote operas without being
operatic composers. The dictum of Mozart after
hearing the young Beethoven—'mark him well, he
will one day get himself talked about in the world'
—may or may not be authentic; it is, however, true
in the semi-aversion which it betrays. On the other
hand we know of Beethoven's pronouncement about
the alleged 'immorality' of the subject of *Don Giovanni,* which may do honor to the man Beethoven
but not to the aestheticist, for the morality of a
piece of music consists only in its quality and perfection. To Beethoven, Mozart must have seemed
conventional; there was no way to connect up with
him. There are few traces of Mozart to be found
in Beethoven, but there are plenty of high-spirited
allusions to Haydn, and rivalries with Haydn.

Was Beethoven a revolutionary? Was he a 'great
man against his time'? Or was he not rather an
executor of his time? The resistance to his works
was astonishingly slight, much slighter than the
corresponding resistance to Haydn. This is not contradicted by the fact that the period had no real
understanding of Beethoven—as we have already
said. People spoke appreciatively about Beethoven,

the 'humorist'; they acknowledged his 'originality.' Beethoven's ill-humor, which his contemporaries took for persecution mania, came from the fact that he did not feel himself to be *properly* understood. But Beethoven did not have to pursue a real struggle against his time. The word 'originality' reconciled his generation to the fact that Beethoven was sometimes an even greater plebeian than Haydn: what was 'naive' in the case of the older man, was rated as 'original' in the younger. Beethoven's aristocratic patrons, too, accepted themes which appear to be intentional insults: completely un-stylized themes like that of the Finale of the piano trio opus 1, No. 3, in C minor, or the one from the Finale of the last piano trio, with its shirt-sleeve vulgarity—a theme which might easily be applied to the words of a coarse but in southern Germany very current request. None of Beethoven's works had to wait for a performance, and each of them was received, if without understanding, at least with respect. Beethoven, as one of the most lonesome of men, wrote in the course of years neither for nor against his time: he wrote for himself and for those unborn generations which would receive his confessions with an open heart.

Wagner and Verdi are the true examples, respec-
tively, of greatness against the time and greatness
with the time. The contrast between the two examples is all the stronger since they were exact contemporaries—born in the same year. Wagner's
greatness: one against all—Verdi's greatness: one
with all, and for all. The one, at the end of his life,
had conquered a world; the other was from his very
beginning so completely carried by the world that
in the end he could offer it even what it did not
like.

The circumstance that Wagner *became* original
saved him from greater opposition at first. *Rienzi*
had a resounding success; Wagner had hit upon
just what German opera audiences demanded at the
time: a historical subject; the tragic demise of a
tenor-hero who was a man of the people and a
democrat to boot; and a Meyerbeerian score, almost
as full of talent as a real one, only in better taste,
cleaner, more homogeneous, less Parisian. The
operas which followed, too—*Dutchman, Tannhäuser, Lohengrin*—roused the ire only of the guild-
conscious critics and of isolated musicians brought
up to other ideals (those of Mozart or Beethoven),
but not the opposition of the public. Schumann

commented on *Tannhäuser* with confusion and obvious dislike (7 August 1847): 'An opera about which one cannot speak so briefly. Certainly it has a whiff of genius [*genialen Anstrich*]. Were he as melodious a musician as he is an ingenious one, he would be the man of his time.'

How mistaken a judgment! Minna Wagner might have spoken like that. Wagner's greatness is based on the fact that he went just the opposite way, that he became more and more 'ingenious' (*geistreich*) and less and less 'melodious.' Yet more and more melodious in *his* sense. How much banality there is, and how much that is almost unbearable not only in *Rienzi*, but also in the *Dutchman*, in *Tannhäuser*, and even in *Lohengrin*. There are revised versions of the *Dutchman* and *Tannhäuser*: Wagner himself felt that his Venus was not equal to the demands of a character that is to be the counterpart to Elizabeth. But *Lohengrin* he never changed, and did not even make alterations in details, because the changes would have revealed too much. His writings are full of aesthetic observations, but sparse in self-criticism: he did not wish people to peek behind the musical *coulisses;* and that is how fat books came to be written about him by people who have not the least relationship to music or anything to do with art. For instance, by Houston Stewart Chamberlain. Wagner's ostensible self-criticism stops with *Lohengrin,* although he certainly would have liked to change many things later on—for instance, just about everything that Elsa sings in her scene with Ortrud, and the all-too-brisk and enthusiastic prelude to the third act. As if to compensate the lack of musical self-criticism, Wagner underpinned few of his works with so much symbolical and psychological meaning as *Lohengrin.*

Today, when Wagner's style has become common property and has found a hundred imitators, we are almost incapable of admiring the consistency and the inventive power which he devoted to the formation of his own personal speech. He knew how radically he was moving away from his time, which at the same time he wanted to conquer—and yet he did it. As an artist he never was untrue to himself. One may permit oneself to be overpowered by his art or one may reject it; but it was *his* art, an art which he created without compromise. Nothing is more worthy of admiration, as a musical, artistic, artistically *moral* deed, than the creation of

Tristan. Tristan was originally conceived by Wagner as an opera that would 'take,' an opera which would provide him, before the completion of the *Ring,* with the necessary means to complete it.

And what he made of it! He made it the work in which his most personal tonal expression finds its culmination; his most uncompromising, and to the average opera-goer most inaccessible work; the work by which he appealed most strongly to the future and to posterity; a work which he himself thought it inappropriate to call a 'music-drama' let alone 'opera'; and which he therefore designated simply as *Handlung*—action—without mentioning music at all. Never was he, as an artist, so lonely as on that 6 August 1859 when he wrote the last note of this score. And with all that he was aware that for the realization of his art—which after all was operatic art and impossible without a 'public'—he needed the co-operation of many people, perhaps all people. Yes, even his contemporaries, if they could be had; for Wagner was not the man to *wait* for posterity. Hence his manifesto to the people, hence the *Meistersinger*. In the *Meistersinger* he created for himself an ideal picture of a public: the people, the naive, uneducated, receptive 'people,' who feel

(243)

the right thing instinctively and receive it with jubilation. Never has the 'people' been more flattered than it was by Hans Sachs-Wagner. If one wants a counterpart to the apotheosis of the people in the *Meistersinger,* let him read the opinion which the other contemporary had about the people:

How touching are thy frolics, oh gentle populace! How sweet are thy pleasures! What poetry in thy sports! What gracious dignity in thy joy! Truly, the great critics are right; art is for everyone. If Raphael painted his divine Madonnas it was because he well knew how exalted is the love of the masses for the beautiful, the ideal, the chaste, the pure. If Michelangelo wrung his immortal Moses from the stubborn marble, if his powerful hands raised a sublime temple, it was doubtless that he might respond to the demand of the masses for great emotions answering to the needs of their souls; and it was to feed the poetic flame which devours them that Tasso and Dante sang their immortal strains. Yes; let all works which are not admired by the masses be anathema! If they scorn them, it is because they are worthless; if they despise them, it is because they are despicable; if they reject them with hisses, let us reject the author likewise, for he is

(244)

lacking in respect for the public; he has outraged its vast intelligence and jarred its deep feelings. Send him to the galleys! *

Wagner himself was often not far removed from this sanguinary irony. The terrible intellectual loneliness, the artistic distress in which he found himself, especially in the years from 1859 and 1864, increased by his material want, were the cause of two moving letters, in which he—and oh! how rarely he did it—finally drops every mask, and gives expression to the whole tragedy which is at the bottom of his struggle, the struggle of the one against his century. Of course he exaggerated absurdly when he painted this century as being beset with all that is bad; and he already had brothers-in-arms a-plenty in his recognition of, and his battle against the middle-class philistinism, the stupidity, and the pettiness of the century: musicians and non-musicians—let us name not only Liszt but also Brahms, let us name not only Schopenhauer but also Nietzsche. The greatest tragedy lay in this— that Wagner himself was far too much caught up

* Berlioz's *Memoirs;* translated by Rachel Holmes and Eleanor Holmes . . . revised by E. Newman, New York, 1935, p.144.

in his century to reap a complete victory over it. He conquered the world; but it was a far too violent conquest to remain undisputed. Wagner's style is a personal style; but an all-too-personal style is carried *ad absurdum* by its imitators. And Wagner's art is —as a complete work of art, and also as the mirror of so latter-day, complicated, many-faced a personality—not pure enough to escape being deified by some and execrated by others. Always he will create parties, and sometimes the one and sometimes the other will be in the majority.

As against Wagner, the conqueror, the musician against his time, we have placed Verdi, *the* musician who is carried by his time and his nation, the musician with and of his time. This, however, is not wholly true, just as the contrary is not *quite* true of Wagner. I recall a questionnaire concerning the relation of the present time to Verdi and to Wagner, and the answer given by a much-admired German conductor, which I should like to quote: 'The comparison between Wagner and Verdi, which people so much like to draw nowadays, characterizes the situation very well. Whatever one may say about the genius of both, it is clear that Verdi is by far the smoother, more directly accessible and

agreeable of the two, not only for singers and other
executive musicians but also for the public. This in
itself already explains in a great measure the contemporary position of Verdi in relation to Wagner
in the public's eyes.'

Both this comparison and this opinion appear indisputable at first sight. But in a deeper sense they
are not 'clear' at all. There is a point of view from
which one need not think of playing Verdi off
against Wagner or Wagner against Verdi; and
from which one may forego depreciating the good
interpreters of Verdi, who are as scarce as the good
interpreters of Wagner—and the true Verdian public, which is as small as the true Wagnerian public.
Verdi smoother, more directly accessible, more
agreeable than Wagner? One might say, on the
contrary, that not only does Wagner's musical ap-
paratus lie much more clearly exposed, but that the
'rational,' the intellectual side of Wagner's creative
act is much easier to grasp than is the case with
Verdi. Yes, Verdi seems 'simpler' than Wagner.
The road to operatic form was straighter and less
complicated for him than for his German contemporary, who had first to erect his own ideal of an
opera, and to settle the musico-dramatic plus the

symphonic concepts within himself. How few predecessors Wagner had! Weber, Marschner, Meyerbeer—hardly Beethoven, and certainly neither Mozart nor Gluck, even if he imagined it. There was German symphony, but hardly German opera. German opera about 1830, when Wagner began, was still a very young creation. How deep, on the other hand, are the roots from which Verdi's opera rose! Opera, and opera alone, was for centuries the real, almost the only Italian art-form, and a straight road leads from Peri's *Euridice* to Alessandro Scarlatti's *Rosaura,* to Rossini's *Mosè,* and from Rossini via Bellini and Donizetti to Verdi. One need only sit in an opera house straightway to enjoy all these operas—no particular 'understanding' seems to be necessary. Nevertheless, I find any given work of Verdi not less full of mysteries than any given work of Wagner; the '*Stride le vampa*' just as interesting as the 'Song to the Evening Star' or Kundry's tale of Herzeleide, the quartet in *Rigoletto* not more 'directly accessible' than the quintet in the *Meistersinger,* an act of *Falstaff* not more 'agreeable' than an act of *Parsifal.*

When one thinks of Verdi, who was carried along by his success in his own time and among his own people, one thinks of *Trovatore* and *Rigoletto* and *Aida*. But Verdi was sometimes an uncomfortable opera composer—even for an Italian audience. His *Macbeth,* to choose an example, is proof that the statement about smoothness and accessibility does not fit—not for an Italian audience, or a German. *Macbeth* was never successful. Not at its first performance, 1847, in the Teatro della Pergola in Florence, where it made only a moderate impression; not at the Scala, where it was murdered by a miserable performance; and not after the revision, in Paris, in 1865. Is *Macbeth* a bad opera? Not at all. Only, to an Italian audience it is a very unpleasing, uncomfortable opera; and to a German or Anglo-Saxon public, which misses the Shakespeare in it, a very contradictory opera—one which awakens mixed feelings. And that sort of thing Verdi wrote, without regard to national success or international success (which to him meant Paris, London, Vienna, and Berlin), not once but several times. Sometimes he tried to save an opera by revision, as in the case of *Macbeth;* but if that did not succeed, he let the opera lie. So he did with *I vespri siciliani, Simone Boccanegra, La forza del destino, Don Carlos.*

But in general it is true that he was carried by the period and the nation. The problems of his operas may be understood, or overlooked, the direct and striking effectiveness of these operas remains unchanged. The average Italian opera-goer does not think about problems when he enjoys *Rigoletto, Trovatore,* or *Aida.* These are works which he can regard as the logical continuation and amplification of operas belonging to a centuries-old tradition; and such, indeed, they are. They are qualitatively better than operas like the miserable *Gioconda* of Ponchielli, which is at least as popular as the *Ballo in Maschera*—but they are of similar kind. The relation between music and stage is in order: which means that the music is everything, the drama nothing. The relation between human voice and instrumental accompaniment is also in order: which means that the orchestra is subordinated to the singers and demands no symphonic preponderance. The action, too, is subordinated to the music; poetry is the 'obedient daughter' of music and supplies to music the impassioned climaxes which it requires for its discharges. Nothing lights up the difference between Wagner and Verdi more sharply than their respective relation to the singers. Verdi makes mighty demands on his singers, and can rarely be satisfied; but his demands are only *more* demands—not different ones from those of Rossini, Bellini, and Donizetti. He was in a position to select the best among the existing international flock of singers, without further ado. Wagner made demands of quite a different sort; he had first to await and educate a new generation of singers for his works, and it was a stroke of luck when he found a willing and intelligent one available.

Only at the end of Verdi's creative work, when he no longer bothered about the 'success' of his works, two more works made their appearance in which besides the musician Verdi there is a little of the poet Shakespeare—*Otello* and *Falstaff*. The difference is clear. What was Schiller in *Giovanna d'Arco* and *Luisa Miller;* what was Victor Hugo in *Rigoletto?* They were nothing but purveyors of the crudest texts. But even in these last two works Verdi remains Italian and traditional: in any case for the historical justification of *Otello* there once was the Florentine *camerata,* and for the justification of *Falstaff* there once was the *opera buffa* of the eighteenth century. And so Italy accepted these last Verdi operas, too, with respectful enthusiasm, al-

(251)

though of course *La Bohème* and *Madama Butterfly* and *Iris* are much more agreeable operas.

○ 8 ○

WAGNER, as the more violent musician of the two, was also more subject to error than Verdi. Music, of course, does not know errors of fact, such as concern the world of science; but there are blind alleys and round-about ways, and miscalculations of one's own powers. In the history of art, for instance, Dürer's visit to Italy, which brought about the influence of the 'renaissance' on his works, is regarded as a false step. With Verdi there are failures, but not errors. Wagner, on the other hand, wrote a work which he himself later described as an error— a 'youthful sin,' namely the opera *Das Liebesverbot.* Here he presumably sailed a false course, under the colors of an allegedly unmoral way of thinking, and accentuated a musical attitude that Wagner, the romanticist, later regarded as unmoral. From the point of view of *Tristan* and *Parsifal* it really *was* an error—a detour into a wrong road. But if it was, then *Rienzi,* too, was a milestone on this false road. A return to the right course—the proper one for

Wagner—came with the writing of *The Flying Dutchman,* and not before. But as a try-out of his dramatic—not musical—talents, the *Liebesverbot* stands as high as *Rienzi,* and even *Tannhäuser.*

It seems that such 'errors' happen more frequently to musicians who are inclined to be romantic than to those who represent the 'classical' type. Bach could never have been thrown off his course; and it would not be correct to regard Handel's operas as a round-about way to his oratorios. Mozart created a hundred minor works, but his path was so straight and intuitive that he was able to fit into his upward course even works which might be called relapses—say, *Così fan tutte,* coming after *Figaro* and *Don Giovanni.*

The situation is quite a different one with Gluck. His 'reform,' in the first place, took the form of a protest and antagonism against the Metastasio ideal of opera. But a year after *Orfeo ed Euridice* he travelled to Bologna in order to compose one of the typical Metastasio librettos, *Il trionfo di Clelia,* and he indulged in such 'relapses' again and again, whenever his circumstances demanded it. He was no doctrinaire, but a *grandseigneur* of art, who could permit himself such things. He turned against his time, but occasionally, too, he went along with it, and with its conventions. His relapses were not errors, but the result of *nonchalance*. And when he wanted to overcome the opposition of his time, he did it with the help of subventions from aristocratic patrons.

On the other hand, the instrumental and dramatic works which owe their existence to Beethoven's patriotism might be regarded as errors, not in the sense of their own time but in that of posterity. They include the *Ruins of Athens; King Stephen, Hungary's first Benefactor;* the Battle Symphony, opus 91; and so forth—works which altogether fill several volumes of the Complete Edition. They might be regarded as errors, because Beethoven was a free musician—the first free musician who could dictate the laws of his time—although he was still sufficiently the child of the eighteenth century not to take the role of an 'occasional' composer too tragically. It was, however, the genuine error of a romantic composer, when Schumann composed his *Genoveva:* it was an unintuitive misconception of his own nature and his powers. He should never have composed an opera at all. Brahms showed a better instinct when he merely *played* with the idea of an opera but never wrote one.

° 9 °

THE nineteenth century, which began to give greater freedom to artists, and especially musicians, then produced the most varied kinds of musicians—musicians who experienced a mixture of contemporary opposition and support. Such decided, if not 'pure,' types as Wagner and Verdi are rare. The particular side of Beethoven's character by which he exercised his most direct influence happened to be in tune with the times, namely the 'revolutionary' and 'pathetic' side. The expressive medium of this revolutionary feeling, in music, is the march—and we know what an important role the march plays in Beethoven's works. This is especially true of his concertos, and there are historical reasons for this. It was the violinist Giovanni Battista Viotti who introduced the march, or rather the march-rhythm, the march-like tempo, into the first movement of the concerto; and Viotti then passed the example on to Mozart. The first movements of several of the most beautiful of Mozart's piano con-

certos (from Köchel No. 415 onwards) are decidedly march-like, and in the Finale of the concerto
Köchel No. 491 Mozart introduced a quick-march,
as Beethoven did later on in the Finale of the *Eroica*
symphony. Amplified and in the end magnificently
idealized, this type of march was incorporated by
Beethoven into the art-form which appealed most
directly to his contemporaries, and with which he
counted on the most immediate effect, namely the
concerto. In the one case where the march element
is less obvious—in the first subject in the G-major
concerto—it had to be made all the more distinct
in the second. With such works Beethoven, as it
were, purchased from his period his charter of freedom—freedom to be as independent as he liked in
his other works, such as the piano sonatas, the cello
sonatas opus 69 and opus 102, and especially in the
quartets; and thus to push courageously forward
into the future.

o IO o

IN the nineteenth century the mutual relationship
between the creative artist and his time changed
every two decades—sometimes even sooner. Mendelssohn had only to write his festive march into

the music for *A Midsummer Night's Dream,* in order to find himself—when Beethoven had only just died—in perfect harmony with his time, a time which, after 1815, was much in need of rest. It is not without reason that Wagner who was a genuine rebel, was so violently opposed to Mendelssohn!

Brahms's relation to his time was remarkable for his time, and also in comparison with Wagner. For inwardly Brahms was much the more independent of the two. Wagner wanted to conquer—and had to conquer—with the heaviest guns, with the mightiest weapons—and conquer he did. But just because of the power and the violence of his conqueror's will, he afterwards had to lose many of those he captured, chained, enchanted, bound. Brahms, on the contrary, waited till the time came to him. He could afford to wait; he knew the influence of his quiet power. Not that he did not find, even in his lifetime, followers and appreciators, beginning with Robert Schumann himself; not that he was not buried with the honors of a Beethoven! He gathered about him a steadily growing community of followers and, with the passing of time, he caught the masses, too. He did not get Wagner's following, for Wagner's influence is international and even extends to France and Italy. But the music of Brahms, too, came to be loved in foreign lands—and if the Anglo-Saxon countries love him differently from Germany, their love is just as deep. Indeed, all who possess a soul, who are sensitive to a completely inward, very intensive, and sentiment-laden music, have followed Brahms.

Brahms was not out to conquer anything, not even the future. Perhaps permanence, but not the future. His music has substance, just as any good, honest, perfect piece of craftsmanship, made from the best materials, has substance. Quite aside from its 'content.' But his music has content, too, which is wholly wrought into this masterly product of his craft—and not only wrought into it but locked up in it. One must find the key. Brahms was an heir—heir to a mighty past. Wagner was stimulated almost exclusively by the present, his own present—after Beethoven and Weber almost only by Marschner, Berlioz, Liszt and—himself. To Brahms the present hardly mattered, except for Chopin and Schumann. Even Schumann, he said, did not teach him much—besides playing chess. But Schubert did—that most captivating of all inventors; Mozart, too, who was so easily imitated

and yet so inimitable; even more Haydn, the primitive and straightforward one; above all Handel
and Bach—and as far back as Heinrich Schütz and
the still remoter masters of the sixteenth and fifteenth centuries.

Brahms knew that he was an heir and nothing
but an heir. But he was not always content to be
just an heir. His beginnings were the beginnings
of storm and stress; up to his first piano concerto
he was, to use Schumann's expression, a 'Beetho-
vener.' The non-success of this work in Leipzig did
not break him, but it changed him. He began to
realize that he could not proceed along this high-
road—the continuation of the past—playing the
equal of the Great Masters. He realized that one
cannot pour out, without further preparation, one's
over-flowing heart. Again and again he shifted
from defiance to resignation, from the spirit of the
C-minor symphony (which Bülow called, because
of its monumental proportions, the 'Tenth'—thus
doing an injustice both to Beethoven and to
Brahms) to the pastoral peace of the second symphony, the pseudo-heroism of the third, and the in-
exorable fate conclusion of the fourth. There are
stations of pure bliss along this road, such as the

early sextets à la Schubert, the late but still Schubertian G-major quintet. In all the categories of his
work—the symphonies, the chamber music, the
songs—we find such stations of happiness. Yet near
the end there are the clarinet sonatas, the clarinet
quintet, in which this happiness becomes a mere
memory: a happiness of the past—one might almost say of the ancient past—lost for all eternity.

Brahms was a humanist. His relation to old music
was similar to the relation of Anselm Feuerbach, his
contemporary among German painters, to the art of
antiquity. Brahms liked Feuerbach, too, as an artist
and as a man: they belong together in the history
of the time. Or we might select a greater example
for comparison with Brahms, namely Nicolas
Poussin, the classicist in whose work all antiquity,
as well as the Italian and French renaissance, are
comprised and dissolved, without detracting in the
least from the greatness of Poussin. Brahms was not
the anti-pope to Wagner, but to Liszt. His name
was the most eminent among all those signatures
affixed to that curious and clumsy protest against
the 'Neo-Germans.' To Brahms these Neo-Germans
did not mean Wagner and his turbulent followers,
but Liszt. Yet he was not really against Liszt's per-

son, but against the alleged formlessness of his music, against Liszt's negation of all that was dear to Brahms in the past, against the *mondaine* attitude of Liszt. Liszt, too, loved Schubert and Beethoven and even Bach, according to his lights (though he despised Handel without limit); but he was not their 'heir.' Brahms was an heir in the highest sense. He did not wish to step out of the frame of the past. It is his glory that he could once again fill that frame—perhaps for the last time—creatively. He did all that was possible—all that was humanly possible—with the situation in which he found himself, namely that he came late, and even a little too late. And so he was and will be understood by all those who also feel a little of the past within themselves—people who also are heirs.

○ II ○

WHETHER a great man is carried by his time, or whether he drags his time after him, his works are always an impulse, a push forward, with which that curious thing known as the world of art (in our case the 'musical world') must come to grips. Musical history—a dubious concept at best—is the upshot of the compromise which arises from the effect of these works on what we call 'the public,' or humanity—an equally dubious concept. If musical history were made by mere talents, the process would be a simple one, and not very dramatic; and as uninteresting as undramatic events usually are. Now there are certain fields from which greatness is *ipso facto* excluded, such as the field of entertainment music—a field with widely separated boundaries, from the popular hit to a certain species of opera. Here the defeat of one up-to-date melody by another is a very peaceful affair, and just as peaceful is the displacement of one popular operetta or musical comedy by another, both being created for 'today.' It would come hard to ascribe greatness to the composer of *Maritana,* or *Martha* or the *Night Camp at Granada.* But 'immortality' has been conceded to some workers in this field, too, as seems to be proved by such names as Lanner, Jacques Offenbach, and Johann Strauss.

The name of Offenbach may even give us pause. Lanner represents merely the musical souvenir of the old pre-revolutionary Vienna; just as Johann Strauss represents the Vienna of the time of Brahms, Bruckner, and Hugo Wolf, which to 'serious' and ambitious people was the guaranty of an easy and comfortable musical existence. One day Johann Strauss will be no more than a musical memento of this Vienna—more durable than that Vienna itself, yet not 'immortal.' But Jacques Offenbach is more than the Paris of Louis Napoleon, and Offenbach's art is a subtler and a tidier art than that of Johann Strauss, in which there is not only the cosmopolitan Vienna which we knew, but the dialect-speaking Vienna of the nineteenth-century boom-time—the greasy, sentimental, smug, conceited industrial town. Offenbach's music, seemingly so dependent upon its own time, reaches out towards regions of perpetuity, yet without any claim to greatness. As always, in the case of contemporaries, Wagner again found the most malicious things to say. In speaking of Auber, Offenbach's rival at the Opéra Comique, he said that Auber's 'cynically pleasurable coldness' and his 'smoothness' were made to cover up 'gracefully hidden dirt.' And of Offenbach, as the exploiter of Auber's style, he said this: 'Here, indeed, we have warmth, the warmth of the dung-heap, in which all the pigs of Europe may roll.' That is a confusion of Offenbach's music and the purpose which it serves. A cultural moralist may talk this way; a musician never. For besides the cheekiest things, graceful even in their cheekiness, Offenbach contains the softest, most tender and most simple details—the most finely cut, and the cleanest, both in the artistic and the moral sense. They are the little flowers on that fabled island of Bimini, of which Heinrich Heine, Offenbach's spiritual relative, sang in a Prologue and three Romanzas, the island which no philistine shall ever be allowed to tread. And it is to these musical blossoms that Offenbach's music owes its durability.

With Giacomo Rossini this durability becomes immortality, in other words greatness—in so far as buffoonery can be great. 'Ecco il *gran* buffone!' The composer of *opera seria*—of *Mosè* or *Semiramide,* the composer of a 'grand opera,' namely *William Tell,* has remained a composer of fashion and a merely historical figure. But the composer of *L'Italiana in Algeri, Cenerentola,* and the *Barber* has attained the heights of greatness—that is, where his buffoonery turns into the unreal, into puppetry, and occasionally into mystery. It is quite a different kind of greatness from that of Mozart's *opera buffa,* but it is greatness, too—greatness in entertainment.

HISTORICAL GREATNESS

This kind of greatness is known only to the con-
noisseur, a man like Verdi, for instance; while
Nietzsche, a man who intimately understood only
Wagner, conceded to Rossini only 'suppleness,' at
any rate not qualities which he expected from his
dreamed-of 'music of the south.' The public, the
masses, also see nothing more in the *Barber* than
amusing diversion. And, conversely, the greatness
of the truly great, from Bach to Beethoven, is only
'greatness on credit' to them. Don't let us make the
mistake to believe that things are different with
Bach, Handel, Haydn, and Mozart than they are
with Dufay, Josquin, Palestrina, Monteverdi, and
Schütz, who are accepted without protest, but as
great historical figures only. Can we really believe
that out of a thousand listeners at a performance of
Bach's *Art of Fugue* (which has achieved a certain
vogue in both hemispheres during the past twenty
years) there are more than three who not only understand this work but take joy in it as well? *Così
fan tutte* is not a lesser masterpiece than *Figaro* or
Don Giovanni, and in the matter of homogeneity of
style perhaps a greater; only Mozart forgot to do
in this, his last buffo opera, what he did in others
—to write for all kinds of ears, with the exception

of long-ears. It is difficult to discover the secret of the dramatic and musical mastery of the *Magic Flute,* and there are many good Wagnerians who are spoiled for such a discovery. What is accessible to the mass is first of all pathos, or—granted!—the power which functions behind the pathos. Otherwise it could not be that Beethoven's Eighth Symphony should lag behind his Fifth in popularity; or the last quartets behind the symphonies. To take another example—it could not be that the Third Symphony of Brahms, which is more characteristic in its pseudo-heroic attitude, should lag behind the First. 'Good Wagnerians' are still spellbound by the seductive demonstrations of the old wizard, and no differently than by the vulgar pathos and the cheap 'tragedy' of Tchaikovsky's symphonic works. Only the consensus of the few determines greatness; those who create, and those who recognize; and those who recognize, which means the true critics, have finer ears and more 'objective' minds than the creative musicians who sit in their cage. From all the world's stupidities, partisan passions, narrow-minded obstinacies, the 'truth' is gradually distilled; that is, the just evaluation of greatness—a truth and an evaluation which are still subject to constant change. And so there exists no eternally valid history of art, no 'objective' history of music; its contents are stirred up again and again, influenced by the ever-quickened sensibility and the intellectual needs of the time. And if ever there should be an objective history of music, we should be justified in assuming that music itself is dead.

This, indeed, is the danger of music in the first half of the twentieth century: that the mutual influence between those who create and those who receive has become so weak. All, or nearly all, musicians of this century seem to have become musicians *against* their time. So much so that they do not seem to count on a 'resonance' for their works—however much they may wish it, and must wish it. They seem to sit, in dreadful solitude, in the well-known ivory tower, donning their own ceremonial garb. The general public rewards them, at best, with indifference, with cold toleration—except for that small circle of interested people who may assume the task of mediating between the artist and the present and—possibly—the future, if they wish.

o 12 o

IF anything is to be said, in closing, about greatness in the present and the future, then the accent should be on this—that music is not yet dead. Our historical knowledge of music is still so unstable, still so much in flux, that one may be reassured about the imminence of music's lethal end. This is arguing by contraries. And that permits us to ask the question: 'Is greatness possible in the field of music, now or in the future?' The only possible answer is a counter-question: 'Why not?' What old Haydn said, at the end of his career, namely that it seemed to him as though nothing had yet been accomplished in his field, and that all the roads into the future lay open, would no longer be quite true today —at least so far as the first part of his pronouncement is concerned. A great deal has indeed been accomplished since then. And as for the second part, we do not know how old or how young the human race is, whether our pessimism has a foundation in fact, or—to echo Goethe—'whether the world, too, is on the decline, because our keg is not running clear.' We *are* pessimistic. Our whole general concept of art has changed. Art today no longer has the meaning it had a century and a half ago, before Beethoven (who was the first to face the world as a 'free creator'), when art was conceived to be an ingredient of life itself, doing service in definite social institutions—the Church, the nobility, a stratum of the middle class. (Only the primitive manifestations of art, those of the child and of the lowliest among the people, have general currency; but whether they are 'art' is a question.) It mattered little in those bygone days, whether the musician permitted his individuality or personality to stand out, more or less, within this social framework; but he could not burst the frame itself; he could not create against the will of Society, or only at the risk of ruin, like Rembrandt, when he no longer hit his patrons' taste.

Once again: art in this sense, as a function and an ornament of life, or, if you will, *only* as function and ornament, no longer exists today. If an artist (in our case a musician) is so wilful as to write works for which there is scarcely a market these days—for instance operas, or symphonies, or songs —he is a very solitary man. The market which still exists is only for forms of music which have a connection with industry, for instance the dance, the film, and the radio. Radio in some cases is also the customer or the distributor of the music of these 'wilful' men; but not because radio loves it, but because it only likes to don a cloak of idealism; and also because its turnover is enormous—so enormous that it cannot do even without the music of the wilful ones. It is the same as when a publisher of popular novels publishes an occasional little volume of poetry, or poetic prose—for the 'honor' of it—and pockets the loss.

I am far from thinking and speaking contemptuously about all music which is in the service of industry. As things are today, it would be at least as important to write good popular music and good background music for films as it is to write good symphonies, string quartets, or operas. Indeed, already in the nineteenth century it was more important to write a good operetta, such as *Périchole,* by Offenbach, than to produce mediocre or imitative operas, such as *Guntram,* by Richard Strauss, *Debora e Jaele,* by Pizzetti, or Joseph Holbrooke's Welsh trilogy. Greatness was possible in both fields —in the one which no longer offered a market, and the one which still has a market—or has one again.

HISTORICAL GREATNESS

But how shall we measure this greatness? How can we say about any particular music of yesterday and today that it must become a permanent possession of humanity? We must leave the question open.

One thing is certain: we are again living in an epoch when musical history has fallen upon hard times. We cannot get around a comparison with the seventeenth century. Then, as now, the old Tablets of the Law had been smashed; today, as then, we are mired in beginnings and experiments; we are fighting to discover a new content and new forms. It is a tragic circumstance at such a turn of events that the last man who is still an 'heir' (and an heir in the long run is always somewhat reactionary) is still happier than the first who breaks the Tablets. One might well cite a dozen examples from all the musical nations of the world, but the most striking, perhaps, is the German one—the juxtaposition of Strauss and Mahler. Strauss was never even conscious of the conflict which came with the turn of the century: quite naively, he regarded himself as the heir, primarily of Liszt, the symphonist, and of Wagner, the mighty one of the orchestral opera; and he quietly continued to plow their furrow. He has been permitted to live very long—which is a gift from Heaven only in the mundane sense. Mahler died young and, like all great men, at the proper time. What, indeed, was there left for him to say, after his Ninth Symphony and the *Song of the Earth?* A tenth symphony was begun, but not finished. In his total symphonic product Mahler gave a complete and exhaustive confession about himself and his time; from this gigantic cycle of music one might reconstruct not only him but the whole strange and mischief-laden period between 1890 and 1914. Mahler, and no other, was the truly representative musician of the time between Wagner and the 'modernists' of today, the time between the hyper-romanticism and the self-destruction of music, the self-destruction which now appears to be a necessity, if we wish to build anew.

It is ridiculous to question the creative power of Mahler because his ideas are alleged to have come to him at second hand. He had exactly the ideas which he needed: like Strauss, he was still one of the last musicians of the epoch which we have first called the romantic, then the hyper-romantic. But he already projected himself into a new one; and like the truthful man and musician that he was, he sensed the break, the conflict, the 'turn.' He was the most contradictory of characters, torn between the extremes of diabolical hardness and angelic soft-ness of heart; of acute neuroticism and serene com-munion with nature; of Dionysian ecstasy and Apollonian calm. His music, too, moves between these extremes. It is the spasm of the music of the last man to be gripped by the great passion, by the great urge to confess, the great suffering, the great love. Then follows the resignation of the *Song of the Earth,* and the raging, destructive negation of the Ninth Symphony. But even in the negation there is despair, and in the resignation there is love—but none of the playfulness, the coldness, the soullessness which came after him, and which had to come. Mahler opened a door to that music by which so-called hyper-romanticism was to be liqui-dated—the music of today. Presumably he would not have understood it. But he might perhaps have understood that this music of today—of the Stra-vinskys, the Schönbergs, the Hindemiths, etc.—could in its turn be liquidated only through a mu-sician who possessed as much love, sincerity, truth-fulness, goodness, and warmth as himself, and at the same time more strength, more unity, and more joyfulness than he.

Whether this musician will come, and when, and in what nation, we do not know. The seventeenth century needed almost eighty years until it could create a new tradition, that is, a musical language in which perfect, legitimate, valid things might once again be said. And in the twentieth century conditions may be even less favorable, although we live faster—or perhaps just *because* we live faster. For in a faster life impressions are always more fleeting, and easier to forget. And how essential it would be to preserve that which is worthy of preservation, and to sink its roots into the earth! Goethe has formulated this so wonderfully in one of the stanzas which were sung at his funeral:

> And thus the living doth new strength acquire,
> From age to age, through ages gone before,
> For 'tis the noble thoughts of steadfast souls
> By which mankind endureth evermore.

We, too, have nothing left but tradition: to draw new strength 'from age to age'—for the greatness which endures. It will be the fate of many musicians of our time to supply the bricks for future edifices, and—at best—to be rated as more or less valuable preparers of the way; perhaps, too, to be found more interesting, more lovable than the consummators, the perfectors; just as the Pre-Raphaelites were once preferred to Raphael himself. For the perfector, again, has the unhappy destiny that he must in turn be 'overcome'; because the history of art never stands still. It is an eternally changeful struggle between tradition and convention, on the one hand, and convention-defying youth on the other. A struggle in which the opposition is always directed against the art of the fathers, and the ideals which are related to this art. In 1900 and thereabouts it went not only against Wagner but against everything that was believed to have a Wagnerian connection—indeed, the whole of romanticism, including the supposedly romantic elements in Beethoven himself. The opposition jumped across Wagner and Beethoven, back to Bach, to the Netherlanders, to the Middle Ages, to everything that was regarded as pure, 'constructive' music; it preferred even the older Bach, the Bach of the *Kunst der Fuge*, to the younger. And another time the whole thing may well happen in reverse.

One is still far from being a 'defeatist' or a 'reactionary' if one recognizes the historical position of music between 1900 and—let us say, 1980, and does not consider it a happy one. Wilhelm Ostwald, a German natural scientist, in a book on *Great Men* (1909) made the remark that 'the purpose of science is to enable man to prophesy.' And if history, which is of course not a genuine or exact science, has any use at all, it is to help us learn from the past and to arrive at conclusions regarding the future trend of events. (Only statesmen are unable or unwilling to learn from the historical past, for the sake of the present and the future.) 'And no study of the past has any meaning,' continues Ostwald, 'if one cannot use . . . the knowledge acquired from the past in order to estimate the future. Thus, for instance, the study of language has . . . no sense, if one cannot make use of it for a better transformation of the language actually in use, whose hopeless inadequacy is hidden from us, or misrepresented to us, by the language experts themselves. On the other hand, the philologists are the most assiduous guardians of the immutability of our language, in other words they are the confirmed enemies of all rational progress. And who does not also recognize, in this essential trait, the essential characteristic of scholasticism?' (Just before the quoted remarks, Ostwald gives it as his opinion that a very great part of contemporary philological and historical science will appear to our grandchildren as medieval scholasticism appears to us.)

It is no different with the language of music. A musician who explains that the language of Bach or Beethoven or Wagner is sufficient for him; a critic who sets himself up as the watchman of the past with its great heritage, and tries to annihilate the present and the future, may as well be thrown on the scrap heap. *Tornare all'antico*—to return to the past, is just as impossible as it would be to take our physical bodies into the times of Bach, Mozart, or Wagner. The language which Bach, Mozart, and Beethoven found and developed was sufficient just for themselves; but there is not enough left of it for us. We must shoulder our destiny; we *must* go forward. We must increase the musical vocabulary, as it has been increased in every period by every master. The unaccustomed and sometimes ugly words of the transitional period will one day seem familiar and expressive. Tradition will transform them.

At this juncture, perhaps, we are forced to think

about the possibility, and the difficulty, of creating a tradition in the twentieth century. This line of thought is not simple. Since this century has rightly been called a machine age, we may perhaps reach our aim most quickly if we compare the tempo of art with the tempo of the machine.

There are people who, out of a certain fear, avoid all visits to a technical museum. (I am one of them.) Partly it may be because they do not consider machine models and tabulations to be proper museum objects; partly, too—and this is my case—because they know so little about anything that has to do with chemical, physical, mathematical formulae, or deals with statics, dynamics, machine construction, electricity, and the production of coal or tar. But one thing even the layman understands, namely the rapidly increasing speed—in geometrical ratio —of all developments in all technical and mechanical fields. In some 'children's corner' of the museum he may see the development of communications, all neatly laid out in a plastic and colorful diorama. He sees how, fifty thousand years ago, a hunter carried his bag of game to his cave—on his shoulders. Then, thirty thousand years ago, the hunter drags it after him, on a web of bast. There he is, ten thousand years ago, pulling it on a wheelcart, or paddling it in a boat. Then follow, maybe three thousand years ago, the pack-waggon and the sail-boat, and so it remains for a time. But the picture changes again after the end of the eighteenth century. Railroad and steamboat appear, and at the end of the nineteenth the automobile and the airplane. The tempo increases constantly, the inventions and improvements fairly chase one another. Records are broken, one after the other. Besides, there are tele-graph and telephone, phonograph, motion picture, radio—the increasing conquest of space, the progres-sive annihilation of distance. And tomorrow, day after tomorrow at the latest, we shall 'televise.'

These are trivial observations, and perhaps not even accurate ones—in so far as the time measure-ment of these historical phases is concerned. And it would be no less trivial to state that we do not know much about the application of these achieve-ments, not even in the technical sense; that for the moment they do not mean much more to us than a precision watch would mean in the hands of a Fiji-Islander; that they have, it is true, brought us some degree of comfort and convenience, but also much killing of soul and destruction, and the threat of

(279)

still more soul-killing and destruction. It would not be any the less trivial to affirm that art has not by a long sight kept step with mechanical development. Not even in the field of musical technique, i.e. virtuosity. Vocal virtuosity has presumably declined since the end of the eighteenth century; the virtuosity of Paganini and Liszt, on the violin and the piano, have hardly been excelled, and only orchestral technique has steadily increased. One perceives that it would be absurd to reproach art for this—more absurd even than if we were to reproach someone for continuing to use his legs, since there are motor cars; or for still using motor cars since he might use a plane.

Art and technique have not the slightest thing to do with one another. The spiritual condition of Goethe and Beethoven did not change in the slightest when they changed from the tinder-box to matches; and the spread of motoring, or the flight of Lindbergh, has made no more difference in the history of art. Art is a district of its own. The best photograph in the world cannot replace the portrait painted by an artist; it is essentially something different. Of course, a picture painted by an artist of today is also something different from one painted in the Middle Ages and down to the threshold of the Renaissance. In those days it was a magical perpetuation, of a personality—holding a personality in ban. Today it is, at best, only an artistic and intellectual perpetuation. A photograph is only a document. Musical works, too, change their meaning in the course of the centuries. A Mass by Palestrina has no longer a function in the Catholic service, in any case not the same function as in the sixteenth century. It is possible today only because the Catholic Church is so friendly to tradition. But in its own day it was much less a 'work of art,' and more a decorative feature of the service; it was, in short, not aesthetically appreciated. This is true, even in much higher degree, of the cantatas or Passions of Bach, which were, around 1730, another form of sermon; a different, more sensual way of interpreting Holy Scripture. Today their value is exclusively aesthetic. The artistic value of a Bach Invention or a fugue is seemingly changed; it is, thanks to its creator, a spiritual mirror, into which we may still look, and into which one may still look after a thousand years. But about 1730 its craftsmanship value was more emphasized; and what Bach particularly wanted to set in motion with the two- and three-

(281)

part Inventions and Symphonies—the stimulus to creative activity—no longer works today; it is as dead as the historically determined form of the fugue. Anyone who composes Inventions and Fugues à la Bach today commits an anachronism.

Once again mechanics and art have nothing to do with one another; they are two separate fields. Mechanics, *per se,* should not be able to harm art in any way. But this is not to be denied: until the opening of the nineteenth century the tempo of their respective development was about the same; but with the speeding-up of the technical tempo there occurs the great break. Art as 'art' became established only in the nineteenth century. Only then did the distant past of art begin to make itself felt, not merely in music, which suddenly began to remind us of Bach and Palestrina; but also in painting and architecture, which only then began to discover the Middle Ages. One might say that 'art,' in our romantic sense, art as a fenced-off area of life; art which is not *used up* in the exalted and solemn moments of life, but which one must enjoy as 'art,' was not invented until the nineteenth century. But Bach, too, hardly ever wrote a work which did not fill its 'practical purpose,' hardly one that he created as an 'art work as such.' Even the Inventions and the *Well-tempered Clavichord* would hardly have been produced, if they had not been justified by their pedagogical quality. The *Art of Fugue* can only be pedagogically explained—as an example of masterly craftsmanship, as a protest against the worthless art of a time which seemed to be getting more and more shallow. That these works incidentally became masterpieces, art works in the purest, most aesthetic sense, is a splendid miracle, but it is not vital. Even with Haydn and Mozart there was hardly a work which was not socially conditioned. Nearly all their compositions were works done to order, works bound to conditions, not 'free' works of art. To neither of these two, nor to any of their contemporaries would it have occurred to write for the 'world'—for an imaginary public. The last three symphonies of Mozart were written for Viennese subscription concerts, which then did not take place, as though destiny had wanted to preserve to them their character as the free products of a high creative power. Nevertheless, they owe their being only to the external occasion. The London Symphonies of Haydn—those upon which his posthumous fame during the nineteenth century

was chiefly founded—would not have been written
had they not been 'ordered.' Brahms's biting answer
to a lady who asked him 'how it happened that he
wrote such beautiful slow movements' has a sem-
blance of historical justification. 'The publishers
order them like that,' he said.

The difficulties of the twentieth century, in comparison with the seventeenth, are further increased
through our intensified consciousness. This difficulty
already existed in the nineteenth century and ham-
pered the creative work of great and little musicians alike. It was necessary to be as great as
Wagner, whose creative power was equal to his intellectual abilities, or, better, who used his phe-
nomenal intellectual faculties in the defense of his
very personal art work, in order to secure the co-
hesion of so doubtful and artificial a building as the
Wagnerian *Gesamt-Kunstwerk*. There was hardly
a single 'naive,' elementary musician left in the
nineteenth century who could practise his handicraft
as ingenuously as it was still possible, or seemed
to be possible, for a painter or a sculptor—say, like
Renoir or Maillol. It is doubtful whether Anton
Bruckner, that curious antithesis, really benefited
from his naïveté. He was a late-comer; and added

to this historical handicap there was his quite un-
commonly slow development and his intellectual
provincialism, which was compensated only by a
deep and explosive emotion and a genuine Catholic
piety. So he stands, like a miracle, this half-medi-
eval, half-baroque peasant of a man and musician,
in the midst of the nineteenth century; and we are
not able to say whether more knowledge might
have enhanced his symphonic form, or whether it
might have done the opposite, or destroyed his being
altogether. The fortunate circumstance that knowledge improves craftsmanship or disappears behind
the craftsmanship has not occurred again since
Schubert's death.

A musician of the earlier centuries existed for the
sake of the Society of his time, but the Society of
his time also existed for him. A Bach cantata had
its own restricted congregation; it did not get beyond St. Thomas's Church in Leipzig. It was intended to be heard once, twice, or three times on a
certain Sunday of the year, and then—to be filed
away. It was neither appreciated nor enjoyed by the
congregation of St. Thomas's, but simply used up.
And that was enough for Bach—in general. He
probably felt it to be a step downward when, after

being a 'princely' Capellmeister, he became a Cantor; but he hardly considered himself to be a misunderstood or unappreciated genius, to whom posterity alone could do justice. His cantatas were just as they had to be. And they had to be good if they were to be worthy of a principal church, such as St. Thomas's happened to be.

Art in this sense, as a component part of life, as a traditional ornament of ecclesiastical or secular solemnity, or more intimate festivities, no longer exists; since the ever-faster mechanical inundation of the nineteenth century. Only since then has art been established as 'art,' namely as a corner of the soul into which we escape from the noise of everyday life—art which is to be enjoyed at music festivals, in concert halls and opera houses. What is true of music is more or less true also of the other arts, and often, too, of the higher forms of poetry, which no longer have any audience at all, owing to the constantly diminishing understanding and appreciation of *form*. It is true of sculpture and painting as well, which have become practically homeless; it is least true, as yet, of architecture. Mechanization, which has transformed our life, has not changed art, but it has changed the conditions in which it exists and the mood with which it must cope. Art in the twentieth century is still cultivated in traditional ways; there are still artists, as there are still savages in Africa or in the South Seas who believe that the sun turns around the earth, and as there are fundamentalists among Christians in Europe and America.

Having mentioned architecture, we may have come close to the solution of our problem. For architecture, as the first among all the arts, is once again occupied with the creation of style. Not by imitation, but through objectivity, by which I mean something quite different than the so-called 'new objectivity.' The most impressive building in New York is Radio City. Is it 'beautiful'? Certainly not in a traditional sense, because it does not trouble itself about tradition and 'beauty.' It has the power and the security of a natural object. I have never felt the desire to ask the name of its creator; indeed, he may remain anonymous to me, like the architect of a Gothic cathedral. (That is the greatest compliment which one can make to an artist.) The building may create a future concept of beauty. Certainly the architect must be familiar with the pyramids of Egypt and the Gothic cathedrals and the dome of

(287)

Michelangelo; but he has forgotten them again, like one who is asleep.

This, too, may be the future path of music and musical greatness. Our great past can no longer be removed from the world—this tremendous spiritual treasure, left to us by a few centuries, and which has sprung from a few of the purest and greatest spirits who have ever lived. Purity and greatness are things too rare to be thrown away. All of the spasms of modern music, the search for new paths, the experimentation—they are futile attempts to ignore the past; futile, because the past cannot be ignored. Or again, there is the attempt to even scores with the past—somehow, in some form; for there are a hundred such forms, and an analysis of them would be a cross-section of the music of today. Great would be he who could comprise the whole past within himself, and be strong enough to forget it again. Happy would be the time in which the forms of art could be *alive* again, like a language which is understood by all—at least by those who have the power to understand.

X